THE COMPLETE GUIDE TO MAKING

MEAD

The ingredients, equipment,
processes, and recipes for
crafting honey wine

STEVE PIATZ

Voyageur
Press

First published in 2014 by Voyageur Press, an imprint of Quarto Publishing Group USA Inc.,
400 First Avenue North, Suite 400, Minneapolis, MN 55401 USA

All photographs by John Barber except where noted.

The information in this book is true and complete to the best of our knowledge. All recommendations are made without any guarantee on the part of the author or Publisher, who also disclaims any liability incurred in connection with the use of this data or specific details.

We recognize, further, that some words, model names, and designations mentioned herein are the property of the trademark holder. We use them for identification purposes only. This is not an official publication.

Voyageur Press titles are also available at discounts in bulk quantity for industrial or sales-promotional use. For details write to Special Sales Manager at Quarto Publishing Group USA Inc., 400 First Avenue North, Suite 400, Minneapolis, MN 55401 USA.

To find out more about our books, visit us online at www.voyageurpress.com.

ISBN: 978-0-7603-4564-1

   Library of Congress Cataloging-in-Publication Data

Piatz, Steve.
  The complete guide to making mead : the ingredients, equipment, processes, and recipes for crafting honey wine / Steve Piatz.
     pages cm
   ISBN 978-0-7603-4564-1 (paperback)
  1. Mead. I. Title.
  TP588.M4P53 2014
  641.2'3--dc23
                          2014002681

Acquisitions Editor: Dennis Pernu
Project Manager: Elizabeth Noll
Design Manager: Cindy Samargia Laun
Cover Designer: Brad Norr
Design and Layout: Simon Larkin

Cover photo © Kellydt/Dreamstime.com

Printed in China

10 9 8 7 6 5 4 3 2 1

CONTENTS

INTRODUCTION

THE FIRST REALLY GOOD MEADS I REMEMBER TASTING were during a presentation by Ken Schramm and Dan McConnell at the American Homebrewers Association's National Homebrewers Conference many years ago. The presentation included samples of a number of meads made with different varietal honeys, as well as a comparison of different yeast strains used in fermenting the same mead. I was hooked on the elegance of good mead. Over the next few years I made a few decent meads, though none was really amazing. In those days documentation on how to make a great mead was hard to come by. Good mead was partially the result of a good recipe but also required a little luck to get a proper fermentation. Ken Schramm's *The Compleat Meadmaker* (2003) sparked new interest in meadmaking and, along with several subsequent articles, led the way to a predictable and repeatable meadmaking process that can produce drinkable meads after months of aging, rather than years.

The meadmaking process emphasized inside this book relies on using the proper amount of healthy yeast at the start of fermentation and adding nutrients to keep the yeast happy during fermentation. Using the right amount of healthy yeast helps you avoid sluggish or stuck fermentations and helps prevent the creation of undesirable aromas and flavors. The book also stresses a no-boil process, no addition of acids at the start of fermentation, and periodic stirring of the must (the honey and water mixture). The process helps you reproduce the same desired results from batch to batch.

The taxonomy of meads featured on these pages matches that used in the preliminary version of the 2014 edition of the Beer Judge Certification Program (BJCP) Style Guidelines. The breakdown developed by the BJCP (which happens to be the most widely used taxonomy) groups similar meads together for judging purposes during competitions and uses the historic names (or one spelling of them) from the Old English descriptions, which is useful when discussing how the meads are made. For some traditional types of meads, the BJCP taxonomy somewhat arbitrarily splits historic categories to make it easier to organize the judging in competitions.

My approach to making meads is fairly rigid in a few areas, including yeast hydration and nutrients, but not so rigid about the exact batch size or even the exact amounts of special ingredients (fruits or spices) added to the fermentation. Since nearly all of a mead's ingredients will have year-to-year and even source-to-source variations, I don't expect the exact same results in two different batches of the same mead made at different times. However, I do expect similar results with regard to the fermentation process and the major aroma and flavor characteristics. I am even willing to blend batches and make other post-fermentation adjustments to get the best mead possible.

The taxonomy of meads in this book matches that used in the preliminary version of the 2014 edition of the Beer Judge Certification Program (BJCP) Style Guidelines, which groups similar meads for judging purposes during competitions.

A BRIEF HISTORY OF MEAD

MEAD IS GENERALLY CONSIDERED THE OLDEST FERMENTED BEVERAGE, since honey—the main ingredient in mead—was the first source of nearly pure sugar. Humans have been hunting for honey for more than eight thousand years. Our ancient ancestors—who didn't have modern tools and techniques with which to extract pure honey from beehives—probably ate a lot of dead bees with their honey. One can imagine the ancients eating the bulk of the honey and putting the remaining honeycomb and debris into a pouch or vessel and later rinsing out the remaining sweetness with some water. Imagine their surprise if the water was left for a few days, resulting in a beverage with some interesting properties. Most likely, pieces of the hive and honeycomb, along with dead bees, would have to be skimmed off the top before drinking this magical elixir.

One can imagine the ancients leaving honey in a pouch or vessel and later rinsing out the remaining sweetness with some water. Imagine their surprise if the water was left for a few days.

As long as five thousand years ago, people in the Egyptian, Greek, and Roman empires made honey wine. More "recently," the Vikings also made honey wine, according to the tales. However, we know little about what this old-time mead tasted like or how it was made. The epic poem *Beowulf* (circa 1000) is one of the oldest writings to mention mead, but the poem doesn't tell us how to make mead.

In 1948 Robert Gayre published *Wassail! In Mazers of Mead: An Account of Mead, Metheglin Sack and Other Ancient Liquors, and of the Mazer Cups Out of Which They Were Drunk, with Some Comment upon the Drinking Customs of Our Forebears*. His book provides a detailed account of references to mead in writings from ancient mythology to modern works. (Beware: Gayre was also a founder and editor of *Mankind Quarterly*, a magazine that was called a "white supremacist journal," among other things.) Gayre wrote that early ale was simply a light mead made from honey but that over time, malted grain was used in production (today, we call this beverage a braggot) and that eventually it became a beverage made entirely from malted grains as a cheap substitute for honey. Gayre also asserted that this early ale was different from modern beer in that it wasn't bitter, since it predated the use of hops in beer.

In *Beowulf*, the grand hall of the king was the Mead-Place or Mead-Hall, implying that mead was for finer or nobler occasions than those that called for ale. Gayre asserted that mead did not become rare because of its quality but rather, at least in part, because of the reduced availability of honey. He lamented the shift in the peasantry to producing mainly sweet sack meads. "This led to the complete neglect which allowed [mead] making not only to pass into the hands of the peasantry entirely," he wrote, "but to remain uninfluenced by the demands of people of taste, and that meant in turn that the liquor degenerated more and more, until the present product made of herbs, hops, spices, honey and even raisins, arose—a shabby pretender never drunk by the gods in Valhalla or by the nobles in Tara's halls." Gayre also argued that the practice of modern beekeepers reusing the combs after removing the honey rather than using the combs to make the drink, as was done in days of old, further reduced the quality of the beverage.

In Gayre's view, mead came first, followed by a lesser beverage made from grapes (wine), and eventually an even lesser beverage made from grains (beer). By his analysis, there came a time when the cost of the ingredients for a batch of mead cost more than the ingredients to make an equivalent amount of grape wine. He was also of the opinion that the Protestant Reformation in the 1500s had a major impact on the availability of honey. Before the Reformation, most European churches needed a lot of wax for their candles, particularly for a High Mass. (He notes one church that used 35,000 pounds of wax a year.) Churches frequently kept beehives to supply their wax; the honey was a useful byproduct that could be made into ale or mead. After the Reformation, churches did not use as many wax candles, hence less need for hives (and less honey as a result).

Gayre also devoted an entire chapter to a discussion of drinking horns, mazers, and mether cups. The Germanic people used decorated drinking horns in the time of Julius Caesar in the first century B.C., and they are said to have been used in England until after the Norman Conquest in the eleventh century. They certainly didn't endure because of their convenience—you couldn't set them down until you emptied them—but because of their ceremonial associations. The early wooden shallow drinking vessels known as mazers were much easier to use. Some say burr maple was the favorite wood for making these vessels, and that their name came from the Middle English word for maple. Mazers were typically made without handles, and some had ornate metal rims. The mether cup was usually four-sided on the top but round on the bottom, with one to four handles. The volume ranged from 1 to 3 pints, and its named derived from the Old English word for mead: *meth*.

Gunlöd, the giantess in charge of the holy mead, serves the Norse god Odin. Robert Gayre bemoaned the denigration of mead by the peasantry to the point that it became "a shabby pretender never drunk by the gods in Valhalla."

One of the oldest works to describe making mead is *The Closet of the Eminently Learned Sir Kenelme Digbie Kt. Opened: Whereby Is Discovered Several Ways for Making Metheglin, Sider, Cherry-Wine, &c. Together with Excellent Directions for Cookery: As Also for Preserving, Conserving, Candying, &c* (1669). As is typical of books from that time, Digbie's work does not include complete instructions or amounts of ingredients, as we would expect today. In fact, many of the "recipes" are no more than a short paragraph of text. For example:

ANOTHER WAY OF MAKING MEATH
Boil Sweet Bryar, Sweet Marjoram, Cloves and Mace in Spring-water, till the water taste of them. To four Gallons of water put one Gallon of honey, and boil it a little to skim and clarifie it. When you are ready to take it from the fire, put in a little Limon-peel, and pour it into a Woodden vessel, and let it stand till it is almost cold. Then put in some Ale-yest, and stir it altogether. So let it stand till next day. Then put a few stoned Raisins of the Sun into every bottle, and pour the Meath upon them. Stop the bottles close, and in a week the Meath will be ready to drink.

CHARACTERISTICS AND VARIETIES

PROFESSIONAL DESCRIPTIONS OF MEADS are characterized by a handful of key parameters, including honey varietal characteristics, sweetness, strength, carbonation, and special ingredients.

CHARACTERISTICS

HONEY VARIETY

Some honeys have strong varietal characteristics, such as aroma, flavor, color, and even acidity. *Varietal* means that the majority of the honey came from a single type of floral source, such as clover flowers. Wildflower honey is *not* a varietal honey, but rather just a generic term used when the floral source is unknown or mixed. The intensity of the aroma and flavor of the mead will vary based on the sweetness, strength, and variety of honey used.

SWEETNESS

Sweetness refers to the residual sugar left after fermentation. In the BJCP taxonomy, meads can be dry, semisweet, or sweet. The body, or viscosity, of the mead is related to sweetness, since increased residual sugar (and thus sweetness) will increase the viscosity. However, sweet meads are not cloyingly sweet and should not taste of unfermented honey. Even dry meads have more body than plain water. Inexperienced tasters may confuse dryness in a mead with fruitiness.

Specific gravity refers to a liquid's density relative to pure water, which is 1.000; final gravity is measured after fermentation is complete. The typical final gravity (FG) of a dry mead falls within the range of 0.990–1.010; a semisweet mead has a final gravity of 1.010–1.025, and a sweet mead runs 1.025–1.050. These are just nominal values, however; other aspects of the mead can influence the perception of sweetness.

Clover is the source of a popular honey varietal.

STRENGTH

Strength refers to the amount of fermentables and therefore the amount of alcohol in the mead. Stronger meads can have more honey character, body, and alcohol than weaker meads, but that is not a requirement and can depend on the variety of honey used and the process. In the BJCP classification, mead strengths are hydromel, standard, and sack, in order of increasing strength.

The typical original gravity (OG) of a hydromel-strength mead (i.e., that gravity measured before fermentation) is 1.035–1.080, and its alcohol level is 3.5–7.5 percent. A standard mead has an original gravity of 1.080–1.120 and an alcohol level of 7.5–14.0 percent. Finally, a sack mead has an original gravity range of 1.120–1.170 and an alcohol level of 14.0–18.0 percent.

The measurements taken with your hydrometer can be used as nominal values to determine sweetness.

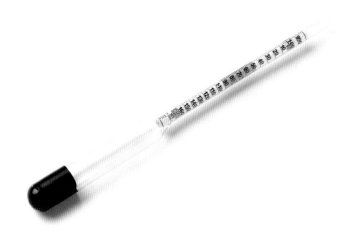

Special ingredients in mead may include fruit, spices, grains, and nuts.

CARBONATION

According to BJCP classification, meads can be still, petillant, or sparkling. A still mead is the flattest of the three, though a few bubbles may be present. Petillant meads are slightly sparkling with moderate carbonation, and sparkling meads are carbonated but not gushing, ranging from beerlike carbonation to that of champagne.

SPECIAL INGREDIENTS

Special ingredients used in a mead may include fruit, spices, grains, nuts, and more (see Chapter 3). Their characteristics may be detectable to varying degrees.

VARIETIES

TRADITIONAL MEAD

The BJCP calls a mead made with honey and water but no spices or fruit a traditional mead. All the fermentable sugars in the traditional mead come from the honey. The subtypes in the traditional mead category—dry, semisweet, and sweet—suggest that the outward difference is in the amount of residual sugar (sweetness) left in the finished mead.

The sweeter versions tend to have increased body (viscosity) as a result of the residual sugars in the finished mead, but this is also influenced by the initial strength. They may also have increased alcohol, but that is not required.

FRUIT MEAD

Within the BJCP taxonomy, meads that include fruit are called melomels. Melomels made from some fruits are so common that subcategories exist just for those fruits. The names of some melomel subcategories follow the historic English names.

The fruit and honey aspects of fruit meads can range from subtle to obvious. Both the fruit character and the honey aspect need to be evident but do not need to dominate. A large range of acceptable levels exists for both the honey and fruit aspects. The fruit character in the melomel needs to be pleasant to support the mead, to be well melded, and to be natural. The balance of the mead may be impacted by the acids and tannins the fruit contributes to the mead, and the color of the melomel may be significantly impacted by the type and quantity of fruit used.

CYSER (APPLE MEAD)

Cyser indicates a mead with apples or apple juice added to the must. Traditionally, a cyser was made by adding honey to apple juice with no additional water. Enough honey needs to be used so that you are not just making a specialty cider (fermented apple juice with a little honey added to boost the alcohol level or to add complexity to the beverage). A cyser needs to be a pleasant blend of honey and apple characteristics. Spices or other ingredients move the beverage into the BJCP's category of Fruit and Spice Mead.

A good cyser takes advantage of the acids and tannins from the apples to create a complex balance. The acids and tannins typically require residual sweetness in the mead to achieve balance, but depending on the characteristics of the apples, dry or even sweet versions can also be balanced.

Apples are a widely grown crop with many varieties. However, most commercially available apples were developed for consumption as raw fruit. Likewise, most apple juices come from a blend of apples meant to create a pleasant sweet beverage. If you can source traditional cider apples or their juice, they work wonderfully in fermented form. Otherwise, you may need to experiment to find an apple that makes a great cyser. Of course, you can add acid and tannin yourself, but the result may not be as complex. A local homebrew club with members who make hard cider may help you find local sources for apples; apples or juices that make good hard cider should generally work well for cyser.

PYMENT (GRAPE MEAD)

A pyment is a melomel made with grapes, generally grape juice. Alternatively, pyment can be made by sweetening a homemade grape wine with honey or by mixing a homemade grape wine with mead after fermentation of both is finished. The BJCP classifies a pyment with added spices (historically called a hippocras) as a Fruit and Spice Mead, not a pyment.

A pyment should be vinous but well melded with a complex balance of sweetness, acidity, tannin, and alcohol working with both the honey and grape aspects of the beverage. Wine or table grapes of any variety or color can be used to make pyment, but most people use wine grapes.

The aromas and flavors of grapes vary from year to year because of variations in seasonal growing conditions; rainfall and temperature have a significant impact on grape characteristics. For most widely grown grape varieties, you can find a range of descriptors for wine made from the grape, but you cannot expect all the descriptors to appear at the same level every year.

European winemakers often name their wines after the region in which the grapes are grown, not after a single grape variety. Although wines may include a blend of grapes from the region, varieties can be restricted. Many wines produced in the United States are varietal wines, made from a single variety of grapes. Pyment can also be made with a single variety of grape, but good pyment (and wine) can also include a blend of grape varieties. Pyment made with a single variety of grape exhibits some aspects of the grape, but since most meadmakers do not process the grapes the same way winemakers do, the mead may not exhibit all characteristics of the varietal wine.

Processing affects the color and other characteristics of wine. Red wines get their color and some other characteristics from contact with the grape skins after crushing. When you separate the grape skins from the juice after pressing, you get a white wine. Pyment makers have the same options, but most pyment makers start with already processed grape juice.

BERRY MEAD

A berry mead is a melomel made from berries. Generally, any fruit with berry in the name fits here, including blackberries, blueberries, chokeberries, cranberries, elderberries, raspberries, and strawberries. Berries can have seeds but they do not have stones or pits. The culinary definition of berry (not the botanical one) is used.

STONE FRUIT MEAD

A stone fruit mead is a melomel made with stone fruits. Generally, any fruit known as a drupe qualifies. Stone fruits are fleshy fruit with a single large pit or stone. Examples include apricots, cherries, chokecherries, plums, nectarines, and peaches. Meads made with a combination of stone fruits are also included. The culinary (not botanical) definition of stone fruit is used.

If you enter your mead in a competition, do not list ingredients not evident in the final mead. For example, if you included a blend of fruits but one is not really distinct, do not mention it on the entry form. If you used a varietal honey but the unique characteristics are not evident, do not mention the honey varietal. The BJCP reminds judges that all the ingredients may not be individually identifiable, but some judges still expect to taste them.

MELOMEL

A BJCP melomel is a fruit mead that does not fit the other fruit mead categories or which is made from a combination of fruits from different fruit categories that takes it outside of a single category. For example, mead made using both grapes and berries, or both berries and stone fruit. The culinary (not botanical) definition of fruit is used.

SPICED MEAD

The spice/fruit/herb/vegetable and honey aspects of these meads can range from subtle to obvious. Both the spice/fruit/herb/vegetable character and the honey aspect need to be evident but do not need to dominate. A large range of acceptable levels exists for both the honey and spice/fruit/herb/vegetable aspects. The spice/fruit/herb/vegetable character in these meads needs to be pleasant, to support the mead, to be well melded, and to be natural. The balance of the mead may be impacted by the acids and tannins the spice/fruit/herb/vegetable contributes to the mead, and the color of the mead may be significantly impacted by the type and quantity of spice/fruit/herb/vegetable used.

FRUIT AND SPICE MEAD

A fruit and spice mead is made with one or more spices and one or more fruits. The culinary (not botanical) definitions of fruit and spice are used.

Beyond what we consider traditional spices, the BJCP taxonomy includes as spices things like flowers (for example, rose petals used in rhodomel), chocolate, coffee, and nuts.

SPICE, HERB, OR VEGETABLE MEAD

A Spice, Herb, or Vegetable mead contains one or more spices, herbs, or vegetables. If a mead only contains spices it is known as a metheglin. The culinary (not botanical) definition of spice, herb, or vegetable is used.

SPECIALTY MEAD

BRAGGOT

A braggot includes grains—typically malted barley, but other grains can be used. Generally, grains need to be malted and mashed as in beer-making, so the complex starches in the grains can be converted into sugars that the yeast can work with during fermentation. Modern beers require hops, but hops are optional in braggot. The grain and honey aspects of braggots can range from subtle to obvious. If hops are used, they do not need to be dominating.

The end result should be a harmonious blend of a wide range of mead and grain characteristics. A braggot is not a honey beer, so it needs to exhibit a balance of both honey and grain aspects.

The spice and honey aspects of metheglins (spiced meads) range from subtle to obvious.

HISTORICAL MEAD

A historical mead is a historical or indigenous mead that doesn't fit into another category. It would include meads like Ethiopian t'ej and many Polish meads.

EXPERIMENTAL MEAD

This mead family serves as a sort of catchall in the BJCP taxonomy. These meads combine ingredients from several other mead categories. Any specialty mead using additional fermentables (maple syrup, molasses, agave nectar), additional ingredients (vegetables, liquors, smoke), alternative processes (e.g. icing, oak aging), or other unusual processes or techniques also go here. Oak aging does not necessarily make a mead "experimental" unless the wood has other characteristics such as spirits (e.g., rum or bourbon). The BJCP says no mead can be out of style for this category unless it would fit into one of the other mead categories.

This category includes braggots that include fruits. Bochet or brochet, a mead made from boiled honey (also referred to as burnt honey mead), uses a boiling process similar to that for making candy. The longer you boil the honey, the darker it will get. If you boil long enough, you will get burnt honey, but before that point you will get different variations of caramelized sugar.

3 INGREDIENTS

ALTHOUGH MOST PEOPLE IMMEDIATELY THINK OF HONEY AT THE MENTION OF MEAD, in fact, special ingredients are often used to make mead. Let's take a look at both honey and special ingredients.

HONEY

Because honey comes from flowers, every batch of honey varies with flower growing conditions. Conditions near the hive can cause bees to forage to different sources than the beekeeper intended. Honey will vary from year to year, from hive to hive, and from beekeeper to beekeeper. Processing of the raw honey can also differ among different beekeepers.

Honey is generally described in terms of color, aroma, and flavor, but the descriptions refer to the honey, and the resulting mead may exhibit different characteristics or a different balance of the same characteristics. Many honey varieties come from the blossoms of common fruit plants, and farmers often pay beekeepers to use their bees to pollinate the crops. Blossoms do not taste or smell like the fruit they produce, so varietals rarely taste like fruit.

The National Honey Board provides good descriptions of the honey at www.honey. com and www.bjcp.org/mead/varietalguide.pdf. Descriptions of mead characteristics of many honeys can be found in the BJCP Mead Exam Study Guide at www.bjcp.org/mead/ Mead_Study.pdf.

Honey derived from the buckwheat flower is a common variety used in meadmaking. It is dark and has the same bold characteristics as buckwheat flour.

COMMON HONEY VARIETIES USED FOR MEADMAKING

Common honeys used for meadmaking are widely available in the United States:

- **Alfalfa:** Very light color and a delicate flavor; it is one of few honey types that leave a slight waxy character in meads made from it.
- **Basswood:** From basswood (linden) tree blossoms; it is very pale and watery and has a distinct, lingering flavor some people find harsh or hot.
- **Buckwheat:** Strong-flavored and dark; it has the bold characteristics of buckwheat flour. The variety from the western United States is claimed to be less intense than the Midwestern version.
- **Clover:** Very widely available and nondescript; its delicate aroma and flavor get overpowered by any strong-flavored ingredients.
- **Mesquite:** Complex, robust, earthy, and raw mesquite character; it is not smoky and works very well with hot peppers and many fruits.
- **Orange blossom:** Typically from orange blossoms but may also include other types of citrus; it has a distinctive aroma and flavor. Its orange character stands up well in meads. Generally, meadmakers consider the California version of higher quality than the Florida version, which seems less fruity, less citrusy, and more muddled.
- **Tupelo:** Light amber honey from the white tupelo tree; it has a very complex and distinctive aroma and flavor, with notes of herbs, wood, and marshmallows. Because of its ratio of fructose to glucose, tupelo honey rarely crystallizes, and the fructose makes the honey very sweet.

UNUSUAL OR RARE HONEY VARIETIES USED FOR MEADMAKING

- **Apple blossom:** Nice floral honey with fairly delicate characteristics.
- **Blackberry blossom:** Fairly distinctive floral, herbal character; it has no overt blackberry fruit character.
- **Blueberry blossom:** Amber-colored, floral, and leafy, with hints of citrus character; it has no overt blueberry fruit character and is not blue or purple.
- **Cotton blossom:** Golden honey with a mild woody aspect.
- **Mint blossom:** White to amber-colored, with a sweet, light mint note.
- **Raspberry blossom:** Golden floral honey with a light citrus background.

DIFFICULT-TO-USE HONEY VARIETIES FOR MEADMAKING

The honeys listed here are difficult for beginners to use in making meads, but not impossible.

- **Pumpkin blossom:** Fairly earthy, to the point of being unpleasant.
- **Fireweed blossom:** Delicate characteristics; it typically takes years to mellow.
- **Heather blossom:** Can make nice mead, but it will typically take years of aging to reach peak condition.
- **Sunflower blossom:** Very indistinct though not unpleasant flavor.

A somewhat unusual variety, honey of the blackberry blossom bears a fairly distinctive floral character with no overt blackberry fruit character.

Fireweed is among the more difficult-to-use honey varieties. Mead made with it can take years to mellow.

SPECIAL INGREDIENTS

Special ingredients include common mead adjuncts such as fruits and spices, as well as less common items like wood and distilled spirits.

FRUITS

Fruits consist mostly of water and actually provide very little sugar. The nondried fruits in the table on page 26 contain about 85 percent water by weight, and the sugar content averages just under 10 percent by weight. The table is derived from data in the U.S. Department of Agriculture (USDA) nutritional database at ndb.nal.usda.gov/ndb/search/list, with values averaged over many samples. While there will be variations based on fruit sources and growing conditions, the table will allow you to determine approximate values for your meads.

For example, adding 15 pounds (6.8 kilograms) of raspberries that are 85.75 percent water to your mead means you are adding approximately 1.54 gallons (5.83 liters) of water as part of the fruit. (Water weighs about 8.33 pounds per gallon or 3.78 kilograms per liter.) The 4.42 percent sugar content means you are adding only about 0.66 pounds or about 10.6 ounces (300 grams) of sugar to your mead.

Taking the water and sugar content of the fruit into account will make it easier to get your mead to finish with the specific gravity you desire. The water in the fruit dilutes the must, and the small amount of sugar in the fruit is not enough to offset the dilution. Most fruits don't give up their water right away when you add the fruit to the must, so you cannot just use your hydrometer to determine the specific gravity. Using 15 pounds (7.03 kilograms) of raspberries in 5 gallons (18.93 liters) of 1.130 original gravity must (before fruit addition) means you are increasing the volume by about 1.54 gallons (5.83 liters) but adding only 0.66 pounds (299 grams) of sugar. The impact is the equivalent of

Calculating Water and Sugar Content (Using Raspberries as an Example)

$$GW = \frac{\left(FW * \frac{PW}{100}\right)}{8.33}$$

FW (fruit weight in pounds) = 15
PW (percent water in fruit) = 85.75
GW = gallons water in fruit

$$GW = 1.544 = \frac{15 * \frac{85.75}{100}}{8.33}$$

In general, fruits with higher acid content, such as currants, create better meads than those with low acid content.

starting the mead with an original gravity of 1.092. A mead with a 1.130 original gravity may finish medium sweet; a mead with a 1.092 original gravity will probably finish dry.

Most fruits contain pectin, a substance in fruit that serves as the gelling agent when making jam or jelly. Pectin in a mead can result in a difficult-to-remove haze, and heating fruit that contains pectin will increase the likelihood of haze because the heat starts to gel the pectin. If you eventually plan to filter the mead, the pectin will plug the filter more rapidly. To avoid creating a pectin haze, you can add some pectinase enzyme to the must with the fruit. Alternatively, you can wait and add the pectinase if the mead does not clarify. Since pectinase (sometimes labeled as pectin enzymes) is available in several forms, follow the package recommendations for the amount to use.

In general, fruits with higher acid content create better meads than those with low acid content. Blends of fruit that taste good together generally make good meads. Some fruits need a little extra processing to create a pleasant mead.

For elderberries, pick the entire head of berries by cutting the head from the plant with a small pruning shears or knife. Put all the heads in a large plastic bag and freeze them, making it easier to extract the juice later. When you're ready to process, let the elderberries defrost and then press them in a small fruit press. You can use the juice immediately or freeze it for later. The stems make up a significant portion of the weight of the head. You don't want all the stem material in your fermenter, or you'll end up with a lot of unpleasant vegetal characteristics in your mead. Note that the leaves and stems of the elderberry are not edible.

Water, Sugar, Acid, and Pectin Content of Fruits

Fruit	Water %	Sugar %	Dominant Acid	Pectin Level
Apple juice	88.24	9.62	Malic	High
Apricots	86.35	9.24	Malic	Low
Bananas	74.91	12.23	Malic, citric	n/a
Blackberries	88.15	4.88	Malic	Low
Blueberries	84.21	9.96	Citric	Medium
Cantaloupe	90.15	7.86	n/a	Low
Cherries, sour	86.12	8.49	Malic	Medium
Cherries, sweet	82.25	12.82	n/a	Medium
Cranberry juice	87.13	12.10	Citric, malic	High
Currants, black	81.96	n/a	Citric	High
Currants, red and white	83.95	7.37	Citric	High
Elderberries	79.80	n/a	Citric	Low
Figs, dried	30.05	47.92	Malic	n/a
Figs, raw	79.11	16.26	Malic	n/a
Gooseberries	87.87	n/a	Citric	High
Grapefuit juice, white	90.00	9.10	Citric	n/a
Grapes, muscadine	84.29	n/a	Tartaric, malic	n/a
Guavas	80.80	8.92	n/a	High
Honeydew	89.82	8.12	n/a	Low
Kiwi	83.07	8.99	Citric	n/a
Lemon juice	92.31	2.52	Citric	High
Lime juice	90.79	1.69	Citric	High
Loganberries, frozen	84.61	7.70	Malic, citric	n/a
Mangos	83.46	13.66	n/a	n/a
Mullberries	87.68	8.10	n/a	n/a
Nectarines	87.59	7.89	Malic	Low
Orange juice	88.30	8.40	Citric	High
Papayas	88.06	7.82	n/a	n/a
Peaches	88.87	8.39	Malic	Low
Pineapple juice	86.37	9.98	Citric	Low
Pineapples, raw	86.00	9.85	Citric	Low
Plums	87.23	9.92	Malic	High
Pomegranate juice	85.95	12.65	n/a	Low
Pomegranates	77.93	13.67	n/a	Low
Prickly pears	87.55	n/a	n/a	n/a
Raspberries	85.75	4.42	Citric	Medium
Rhubarb	93.61	1.10	Malic, oxalic	Medium
Strawberries	90.95	4.89	Citric	Low
Tangerine juice	88.90	9.90	Citric	n/a
Watermelon	91.45	6.20	n/a	Low

Source: USDA Nutritional Database

Use a small fruit press to process berries that you've just picked or have stored in your freezer. You can use the juice immediately.

While rhubarb stalks contain a lot of water, pressing them fresh doesn't work well. However, you can cut the stalks into workable chunks and freeze them in plastic bags, which really seems to break down rhubarb. You can then defrost and add the rhubarb to your fermenter.

Chokecherries are very astringent (high in tannins) fruits traditionally used for jams, jellies, and fruit wines. Well-ripened berries will be less astringent, and aging the chokecherries for a day or two in the refrigerator after picking will also soften the astringency. Simmer the chokecherries in just enough water to cover until they are soft and release their juice to the water, then strain the pulp to extract the juice for meadmaking. One gallon of chokecherries yields about 1.5 quarts of juice.

Many varieties of *chokeberries*, similar to chokecherries, will have earthy characteristics when picked, but cooking the berries seems to significantly reduce or even eliminate this characteristic. Place the berries in a pot and add enough water to just cover them. Boil 20–30 minutes, until the berries begin breaking down. Strain to remove the juice—a jelly strainer or a large funnel lined with cheesecloth will work. Cool the berries to room temperature if using immediately or freeze the juice for later. Like chokecherries, chokeberries are very astringent.

Wild grapevines produce small berries and are extremely sour; without adjustment, the acid levels are too high to make reasonable mead with. However, home winemakers have found techniques that reduce the acid levels. With the exception of the fox grape (*Vitis labrusca*) and the muscadine grape (*V. rotundifolia*), these techniques are useful for all North American wild grapes (generally *V. riparia*). After harvesting whole clusters

Many varieties of chokeberries have earthy characteristics when freshly picked. Cooking seems to significantly reduce or even eliminate this quality.

from the plants, gently crush the grapes with the stems attached, but don't crush the seeds. Pour the crushed grapes into a mesh bag and wring out the juice, a dark purple juice very high in tartaric acid. Wear rubber gloves to prevent the juice from soaking onto your skin, or it will burn for several hours. Limited contact is fine, but extended contact is painful. Store the juice in the refrigerator for a couple of days, and the tartate will settle into a gray sludge. You can then pour the juice off the sludge to reduce the tartate content. You will lose around one-quarter to one-third of the juice in the process.

FRESH FRUITS

Freshly picked fruits are the first choice for high-quality melomels. You-pick farms, local food stores in season, and local farmers' markets serve as sources for really fresh fruit. You want your fruit to be clean and free from debris, leaves, and insects. Place fresh-picked berries in a clean sink full of cool water, and lots of the debris will float to the top. Carefully use your hands to remove the berries; eliminate the unripe or damaged fruit. Some fruits, such as raspberries, are fairly delicate and can be hard to wash without smashing; for these it is best to just run water over a handful at a time to wash them.

I once made a mead with over 25 pounds of fresh strawberries in it. After washing all the fruit, I spent a lot of time cutting off the green leafy tops. Later, while chatting with Jon Hamilton of White Winter Winery, I mentioned how much work that was. He said to not bother with it; just put the fruit into the fermenter, and it won't matter in the end. At White Winter Winery, they try to time their production of fruit meads to match up with the local fruit harvest, so they can use fresh fruit.

FROZEN FRUITS

Sometimes I can't find the fresh fruit I want or don't have time or fermenter space to make the mead at the time the fruit is available. Using commercially frozen fruit or freezing fresh fruit can solve the availability issue. Your local grocery store may have a selection of frozen fruits, but if not, some of the big-box discount stores will.

Many people think freezing will sanitize fruit, but it won't. A freezer preserves fruit because it significantly slows down decay and keeps wild yeasts and bacteria dormant. However, once the temperature is increased, those wild yeasts and bacteria wake up.

Freezing fruit before fermenting can even be an advantage with some fruits. Freezing helps break down the structure of the fruit and make it more accessible to the yeast during fermentation. Freezer burn (a result of dehydration and oxidation) may be more recognizable on things like meat, but it can also happen to fruits. The unpleasant flavors and aromas that result cannot be removed from the fruit and will carry over into the mead. You can minimize the problem by freezing the fruit in a bag designated as a freezer bag, which generally means it is thicker and seals better than your average sandwich bag. Long-term storage in the freezer increases the chance for freezer burn, so don't leave your fruit in the freezer for years and expect it to taste fresh when it's defrosted.

To help stave off the oxidation, I lightly spray fruit I am going to freeze with a concentrated solution of sulfite. Make up a solution by mixing 50 grams (approximately 8 teaspoons or 1.76 ounces by weight) of potassium metabisulfite in 500 milliliters (16.6 ounces) of water. Shake to dissolve.

Commercially frozen fruits can also suffer from freezer burn. Bags with even a pinhole in them are more susceptible, since the hole allows dehydration and oxidation to start.

JUICES AND CONCENTRATES

You can find many fruits in juice or concentrate form at your local grocery store, although you do need to read the label to verify the ingredients. You generally do not want juice sweetened with sugars or artificial sweeteners. Some juices are sweetened with apple or white grape juice, and while those sweeteners are natural and fruit-based they won't add much, if anything, to your mead. Try to find juices that have nothing but the original fruit, and skip juices with preservatives added to avoid stifling the fermentation. Pasteurized juices are fine to use, although the heating process does take a little character out of the fruit. Your hydrometer will tell you how much sugar the juice contains.

I have had good luck with a few fruit juice concentrates, typically those purchased from the grower, including raspberry, pomegranate, blueberry, and cherry concentrates from a variety of vendors. Concentrates with an eight-to-one ratio—where 1 quart of the concentrate equals 2 gallons of fresh juice—tend to be relatively free of solids and pulp, meaning using them in your mead will not leave a lot of fruit sediment at the bottom of the fermenter. Your hydrometer will tell you how much sugar is in the concentrate. The water percentage table on page 26 will help you approximate how much fruit went into the concentrate. For example, one quart (0.95 liter) of raspberry concentrate at 8:1 would be two gallons (7.57 liters) of juice or about 16.7 pounds (7.56 kg) of water. Given that raspberries are approximately 87.75 percent water, you would need around 19.5 pounds (8.85 kilograms) of berries to get the equivalent liquid in your mead. (Of course, this is an approximation, since the concentrate maker cannot get all the water or sugar out of the fruit.)

During the wine grape harvest, a number of fresh grape juices derived from the *V. vinifera* species are available for making pyments. These juices may be a little harder to locate, but your local homebrew supply store may be able to get them for you, or you can check with members of local home winemaking clubs to see if members have a source. The juices are generally shipped right after the grapes are pressed, have no preservatives added, and need to be shipped refrigerated. Even when shipped refrigerated, the juices may still have some slight fermentation underway when they arrive. White, rose, and red grape juices are usually available and will typically have an original gravity in the 1.090–1.105 range, depending on the grape variety and the growing season. The juice usually comes in a 6-gallon bucket, so I will typically freeze a couple of gallons of the juice in plastic jugs. The frozen juice comes in handy if you want to back-sweeten your mead after fermentation.

PURÉES

A number of fruits are available as aseptic purées, typically packaged in large cans or possibly large Mylar bags. They require no refrigeration and have a long shelf life if unopened, making them convenient for the meadmaker. The characteristics of the fruit, however, tend to be more subdued than those of fresh fruit or even most frozen fruit. All the fruit has essentially been ground up, so it will all settle to the bottom of your fermenter at the end of fermentation. After using more than 20 pounds (9.07 kilograms) of purée in a batch, I've ended up with several gallons of fruit-based sludge at the bottom of the carboy that is nearly impossible to separate from the liquid.

In some purées (especially with stone fruits like peaches and apricots), I have also found a taste that reminds me of biting into an unripe peach or apricot, but since all the fruit has been puréed, you can't separate out the unripe fruit before adding it to your fermenter. Still, that may be a tradeoff you are willing to make for the sake of convenience.

WINE KITS

The typical homebrew supply store will have a wide range of wine ingredient kits—not just grape wine kits but even fruit wine kits and ingredients. Grape wine kits can be a great source for juice to make a pyment. Many modern grape wine kits come packaged with 6 gallons of grape juice.

I use only the fruit portions of wine grape kits, discarding the other ingredients, and I especially don't use the yeast if the kit includes one. The kit may include the grape skins, useful for more authentic character from red wine varieties, and it may also include a second packet of juice. (I add it a day or two into the fermentation.)

Fruit wine kits consist mainly of cans of fruit or fruit juice concentrate that range from cherry and raspberry to elderberry and marionberry. The best kits are all fruit and have no sugar added.

OTHER INGREDIENTS

SPICES

Since we are following the BJCP taxonomy of meads, our spice definition for metheglins is more liberal than a true botanical definition. Spices also include herbs, vegetables, and other ingredients. Spices include allspice, black pepper, cardamom, chamomile, chocolate, cinnamon, cloves, coffee, coriander, ginger, hot peppers, lavender, lemongrass, mint, nutmeg, orange peel, rose petals, rosemary, saffron, star anise, and vanilla.

Some spices work in isolation better than others do. For example, ginger works well as the only spice, but nutmeg seems to work better in a blend of spices. There is no definitive right or wrong spice or spice blend; your preferences drive your ingredient selection. When experimenting, you should use less of the spice than you think is required. You can always add more, but it is hard to remove excessive spices.

Spices are agricultural products and will vary from year to year and from region to region. Spices deteriorate with age, and improper storage conditions will accelerate the deterioration. When making a metheglin, I use quality spices from a quality supplier, who can typically provide things like multiple kinds of cinnamon, different types of peppercorns, and several varieties of hot peppers.

Spices work well in more than just metheglins. But when spices are added to other fruit meads, the meads belong to the spice, herb or vegetable category. I added cinnamon to a cherry melomel that was too sweet, which increased the tannin level and had a positive impact on the overall balance. Adding a blend of mulling spices to a pyment can create a similar character. Some fruits seem to improve with a subtle addition of spice—for example, a hint of vanilla seems to intensify the characteristics of cherries, cinnamon goes nicely with the apples in many cysers, and chipotles go well with raspberries.

I find it easier to add spices after the vigorous part of the fermentation is over. You can add them right from the start, but the spices can get a little messy when you need to stir the mead. To solve this problem, put all the spices in a small mesh bag and remove it for stirring. The mesh bag must be sanitary, but I don't use chemical sanitizers on fabric. I boil the bag for a few minutes in just enough water to cover it.

I sanitize spices with cheap vodka: I mist small loose spices with a spray bottle of vodka and let them sit for a few minutes, and I cover ground spices with vodka in a small jar. Larger spices can be immersed in a small jar or plastic bag of vodka for a few minutes, and if the vodka picks up much of the spice character, I add that to the fermenter along with the spices.

The essential characteristics of spices are extracted differently in water, in alcohol, in oil, and with heat. (Cooking oil doesn't work well in meads.) When you add a spice to a mead, you are getting some extraction in water and some in alcohol. If you want to use heat extraction, you will need to do that in advance. You can boil the spices in a little water and then add that water and the spices to the fermenter. You can increase alcohol extraction by steeping the spices in a small amount of cheap vodka in a sealed jar for a few days before adding the vodka and spice to the fermenter.

Raw ginger can have an intense flavor. Used correctly, though, it can result in a mead that reminds one of an adult (i.e., alcoholic) form of old-fashioned ginger ale.

GINGER

This popular root is readily available year-round, and many food stores sell it raw in bulk. You can also buy candied ginger (which has been cooked with sugar until soft) or crystallized ginger, but the flavor difference between the raw and candied forms is significant. Candied ginger has a softer flavor, like spicy candy. Raw ginger can be so intense that you may not even want to bite into it. If you can't find candied ginger, you can find many recipes for making your own.

I frequently use several pounds of ginger in a batch of mead. My ginger mead that won the AHA Meadmaker of the Year Award in 2008 had well over 3 pounds (1.36 kilograms) of raw ginger in 5 gallons (18.93 liters) of mead. It was sort of like an adult (alcoholic) form of old-fashioned ginger ale. I initially peeled the ginger, but since that gets really tedious with so much ginger, I no longer bother with peeling. I do cut it into thin slices using a food processor, put all the slices into a sanitized mesh bag, and throw the bag into the fermenter right from the start.

Dried peppers are more pleasant in a mead because they tend to give off fewer vegetal notes.

HOT PEPPERS

When using hot peppers, I find the dried ones more pleasant in a mead because they tend to give off fewer vegetal notes. The chef's technique of browning dried peppers 20–30 seconds in a hot, dry frying pan can enhance the character; you just want to get a few brown

Cocoa nibs are the best chocolate for mead. Add after the vigorous part of fermentation to avoid a mess when stirring.

spots on each side of the pepper. Blending varieties of hot peppers tends to increase the complexity over a single variety of pepper. Beware: peppers can easily overwhelm the mead, so start with much less than you think will be needed and adjust later.

COFFEE

I'm not a big fan of coffee meads, but if you use coffee, avoid boiling it. The good coffee meads I have tasted were generally made with cold-pressed coffee, which seems to prevent harshness.

MINT

When I use mint, I have more consistent results with dried mint than with fresh mint, perhaps because the dried form is more consistently grown and harvested. Mint can be used as a delicate or dominant ingredient. I've won medals with a sweet mead that had a pound of dried spearmint leaves, so there was no missing the mint in that one.

CHOCOLATE

If you're going for chocolate, cocoa nibs are your best choice. Add after the vigorous part of fermentation has been completed to avoid making a mess when stirring the mead. Chocolate will leave a little cocoa fat floating on the top of the fermenter. You'll want to leave the fat behind when you transfer the mead.

FLOWERS

Many flowers will contribute pleasant floral characteristics. Just make sure the blossoms are edible before you use them. Flowers used in making various tea blends (chamomile, hibiscus, rose, jasmine, lavender) tend to be safe choices. With flowers, you may find extracting the petals from the blossom head reduces the vegetal characteristics that come from the green parts of the blossom. See the opposite page for examples of edible flowers, as well as their characteristics.

If you plan to use rose petals, you need to be sure they are edible. While you can find a lot of loose rose petals at the end of the day in a flower market, they probably were treated with various toxic insecticides and fertilizers. As alternatives, you can buy some rose blossom teas, use food-grade rose water, or grow your own roses.

Bergamot, commonly called bee balm, is a natural choice for meads, since bees love it. The leaves of the plant have a light mint character. Harvest the blossoms, extract the petals, sanitize them with vodka, and then add both the petals and the vodka to the mead. A few ounces of the petals will impart a noticeable floral and minty note to a mead. Late-season wildflower honey often seems to carry a note of bergamot naturally, since bergamot blooms in late summer.

Small cubes of oak at different toast levels can be used to change the flavor and aroma characteristics of mead. But be careful! The use of wood in mead is an art—you will need to monitor the mead frequently to make sure you don't get too much wood character.

WOOD

Different wood species will impart different characteristics to mead, and wood can be added through several different means. Wood adjuncts were also developed for winemakers and can be used in the typical carboys. Wooden barrels are used in both the wine industry and for some distilled spirits.

The use of wood in mead is an art—you will need to monitor the mead frequently to make sure you don't get too much wood character. Wood will add tannins and other flavors and aromas, influenced significantly by the species and processing of the wood. While the common wood species in winemaking are American, French, and Hungarian oak, some craft breweries have experimented with other species, including Florida's Cigar City Brewing, which has produced beers using orange, lemon, and even Spanish cedar wood.

Small cubes and chips of several different types of oak (American, French, and Hungarian) at different toast levels (heavy, medium plus, medium, and light) were developed as an alternative to barrel aging in home winemaking. These can also change the flavor and aroma characteristics of mead. Wood spirals and honeycombs processed in bigger pieces will still fit into a carboy and

Apple blossom: delicate floral notes.

Carnation: spicy, peppery, clovelike.

Citrus blossom: waxy citrus flavor.

Chrysanthemum: pungent and musky.

Clover: sweet and aniselike.

Hibiscus: slightly acidic.

Hollyhock: bland flavor.

Lavender: floral and perfumey.

Lilac: lemony and floral.

Marigold: spicy and bitter.

Pansy: mild, sweet, and tart.

Violet: sweet.

are available in more species than cubes—for example, I've used cherry wood and maple spirals and honeycombs.

Chips release their character the fastest, followed by honeycombs and spirals, and then cubes. Oak toast levels are described as follows:

- **Heavy:** rich, carmelized, carbonized, smoky, espresso
- **Medium plus:** honey, roasted nuts, low coffee, vanilla, spices
- **Medium:** warm, sweet character with strong vanilla and caramel— more aroma than flavor
- **Light:** fresh oak, coconut, fruits

Note that chips, cubes, spirals, and honeycombs need to be sanitized before going into the mead. I don't use chemical sanitizers on porous things like wood. Instead, I use immersion, complete saturation, or hand spraying with a cheap vodka. Five minutes of contact time is generally effective.

Because it may be hard to assess the appropriate time to remove the wood while the mead is still developing, I prefer to add it after fermentation. Periodic sampling is essential to avoiding too much wood character. Use a wine thief (a long tube inserted through the small neck of the carboy to extract a sample) to sample from a carboy or draw a small sample via a tap if your mead is in a keg. In either case, remove the wood quickly once the proper level is reached—I prefer to stop a little on the light side and then create a tincture from the wood at packaging time if necessary.

Barrels: Barrels introduce another level of character to the mead. You can purchase a new barrel in the typical winemakers' toast levels made from the typical species of wood, or you can buy a used barrel. Used barrels may have contained wine, whiskey, rum, cognac, or something else and can impart extra character from the previous beverage. Used barrels are also large; commercial wine barrels generally hold 59 gallons (223.3 liters), and whiskey barrels are typically 53 gallons (200.6 liters). These are really big barrels for the home meadmaker. You might try to interest a bunch of fellow meadmakers in filling the barrel together. Demand for smaller used barrels generally exceeds supply.

New barrels will mainly impart the same characteristics as chips, cubes, spirals, and honeycombs of the same wood species. The barrel lets oxygen in while the mead is aging, oxidation that can introduce subtle changes in the flavor and aroma, softening the tannins and increasing the complexity of the fruity notes.

I do not ferment in a barrel. Instead, I fill the barrel with mead that has finished fermenting and is generally clear. Barrels will lose (evaporate) some of the water and even alcohol from the contents during aging, an amount called the "angel's share" in the whiskey business. You need to plan ahead to have sufficient mead available to periodically top up the barrel during aging and to replace the amount you remove during sampling. The typical angel's share is 1–3 percent of volume per year.

You can use monofilament fishing line or unflavored dental floss to suspend a spiral or honeycomb in your fermenter. Tie one end to the wood and then lower it into the carboy. The line or floss will not prevent the stopper from sealing the carboy.

Topping up the barrel helps protect the barrel and the beverage. It prevents the barrel from drying out and losing its liquid tightness. Extra headspace can increase the oxidation rate and allow detrimental organisms to grow.

Because of the increased surface-to-volume ratio, smaller barrels tend to give their wood characteristics to the mead much faster than large barrels do. Smaller used barrels will pick up previous beverage notes more quickly as well.

You need to be very careful with sanitation when opening a barrel for sampling or topping up. I spray the area around the opening with vodka a few minutes before opening. Before filling the barrel, you can also drill a small hole in the head that can be tightly plugged with a stainless steel nail. Removing the nail will allow a slow stream of mead to run out that can be stopped by reinserting the (resanitized) nail.

DISTILLED SPIRITS

The addition of distilled spirits to mead is somewhat akin to making port. You can add neutral spirits (you want to use the highest percentage alcohol you can get to minimize the water addition) to a mead to increase the alcohol level, but if you increase the alcohol level beyond the tolerance level of the yeast, you will stop the fermentation (generally 15 to 20 percent alcohol). The port maker's art is to know when in the fermentation (at what residual sugar level) the wine is going to taste best when the alcohol is increased. One way to accomplish this is by doing small-scale experiments in which you carefully measure the mead and then add measured alcohol to see if you are ready to stop fermentation. Then you can use a Pearson's square (see Chapter 8) to determine how much spirit to add.

Barrels introduce another level of character to mead. Used barrels may have contained wine, whiskey, rum, cognac, or something else and can impart extra character.

You can also add distilled spirits just to increase the alcohol level without trying to stop fermentation if you feel that would be an appropriate balance adjustment.

An interesting meadlike beverage that depends on distilled spirits is Xtabentún, an anise-flavored liqueur made in the Yucatan region of Mexico. Xtabentún is made from anise seeds and honey from the nectar of the xtabentún flower (Mexican bindweed), a member of the morning glory family. The seeds of xtabentún are said to be a natural source of the hallucinogenic drug LSD and were supposedly used in religious ceremonies by the Aztecs and subsequent indigenous cultures. Xtabentún is fortified with rum to around 20–30 percent alcohol by volume (ABV). Since commercial examples are deep yellow and sometimes have a green tint, it would seem a light (clear) rum is used. An exceptionally sweet, aniselike liqueur, xtabentún uses anise and alcohol to balance its high residual sugar content.

YEAST STRAINS

ALTHOUGH MEADMAKERS HAVE MANY YEAST STRAINS TO CHOOSE FROM, it may be best to begin with just one or a few until the process is comfortable. You can then introduce different yeast choices to expand the characteristics of your meads.

Most strains are sold as wine yeast, with only a handful called mead yeasts. Beyond these classic strains for wine and mead, you can also consider some of the beer yeast strains. Beer strains are generally well characterized for aroma and flavor characteristics they produce in beer; their performance in mead will be similar, but the must will not have the same constituents as beer wort, resulting in slightly different fermentation characteristics.

YEAST PACKAGING

While many yeast vendors provide products that can be used for meadmaking, the yeast comes in either a dried (dehydrated) or liquid form. Neither form is ready to use if you want the best results. The dried yeast needs to be rehydrated, and liquid yeast packages typically do not contain nearly enough yeast for a batch of mead; you need to grow more yeast using a starter.

REHYDRATING DRIED YEAST

The process of rehydrating dried yeast does not involve growing more yeast cells, as you do with a liquid starter. While you can use a starter with a dried yeast strain after it has been rehydrated, most people don't because the packets are fairly cheap. Rehydration takes only a few minutes, while a starter can require a day or two to be ready to use.

Dried yeast has a very long storage life. Some vendors encourage freezer storage of unopened packets. Frozen yeast must be allowed to revert to room temperature and rehydrated before it can return to its normal active form.

During the first few minutes of rehydration, the yeast goes through a stressful transformation from dry to normal working form. The yeast cells take up minerals from the rehydration liquid, so rehydration in distilled or deionized water is not recommended; it can be lethal to the yeast. Yeast vendor Lallemand suggests that 250 parts per million (ppm) of hardness in the rehydration liquid is ideal. Rehydration in cool water is not recommended. Rehydration in 60°F (15.6°C) water can result in a 60 percent reduction in the viability of yeast cells, so most dried yeast vendors recommend a temperature of around 104°F (40°C).

Lallemand worked with other researchers to develop the rehydration nutrient Go-Ferm to help prevent sluggish or stuck fermentations, those that take too long or never reach the intended final specific gravity. To rehydrate dried yeast, start by sanitizing a glass container such as a measuring cup or a pint glass. For a 4-gram package of dried yeast, you need 5 grams (0.011 pound or 0.176 ounce by weight) of Go-Ferm (1.25 times the weight of the yeast) and approximately 4 ounces of water (approximately 25 times the weight of the yeast). Place the water (approximately 104°F [40°C], use the temperature recommended by the yeast vendor) in the glass, add the Go-Ferm, and stir to dissolve. Add the yeast, stir gently to suspend, and wait 15–30 minutes for rehydration. Waiting more than 30 minutes will result in a decline in the yeast population. I cover the glass with plastic cling wrap during the rehydration to keep wild yeast and bacteria out.

USING A LIQUID STARTER

Liquid yeast sources are typically viable in the vendor's container, but the container does not hold sufficient yeast cells for the original gravity and batch sizes of mead, so a yeast starter is necessary to grow more.

In my mead, I use starters made with preservative-free apple juice from the grocery store. (Look for pasteurized juice, because added preservatives may prevent the yeast from growing.) I grow my starters in a flask on a stir plate. The Mr. Malty calculator (www.mrmalty.com/calc/calc.html) shows that a stir plate greatly reduces the size of the starter you need to grow enough yeast.

One U.S. fluid ounce of pure water equals about 29.5 grams. A good approximation for the amount of water to use during rehydration is 1 U.S. fluid ounce per gram of dried yeast.

I get my starter going a couple of days before I plan to brew. Starters on a stir plate typically finish growing after about 24 hours, and at that point I turn the stir plate off and let the yeast settle to the bottom. Just before I pitch the starter into the must, I decant most of the liquid off the top, leaving the yeast slurry. I then swirl the starter flask to get the yeast resuspended in the remaining starter liquid and pour the starter into the fermenter while holding a permanent magnet outside the flask to keep the stir bar from going in. If the yeast starter is warmer than the must, the atemperation steps described in Chapter 6 must be followed. I do the atemperation after the bulk of the starter liquid is decanted off the starter.

You can grow a simple starter without a stir plate, but you will need a larger vessel such as a glass gallon jug. Because of the large volume of liquid in the simple starter, you really need to decant the liquid off the yeast; you don't want to dilute your mead with the starter liquid. You need to begin the starter several days before you mix the must and allow time for the yeast to grow, since it takes longer in the simple starter than on a stir plate. After the growth has stopped (when the starter is no longer bubbling), let the yeast settle to the bottom of the jug. Then decant most of the liquid off the top, swirl the jug to get the yeast resuspended in the liquid, and pour the result into the must.

MEAD AND WINE YEASTS

The yeast strain descriptions below are based on data from various yeast suppliers, but the vendors did not all provide the same kinds of information. Terms like *medium nitrogen requirement* or *high ester production* are useful when comparing strains from the same vendor, but comparing such terms may not work across vendors. The nitrogen requirement is generally fulfilled by the staggered nutrient additions (see Chapter 5); strains that call for a high level of nitrogen may require more than the typical dosage.

The yeasts in the following chart are basically the same, but there may be slight differences between vendors.

Mead and Wine Yeasts	
Name	Sources
Assmanshaussen	White Labs WLP749, Enoferm Assmanshausen
Bourgorouge	Lalvin RC212, White Labs WLP760
Pasteur Red	Red Star Pasteur Red, Wyeast 4028, White Labs WLP750
Pasteur Champagne	Red Star Champagne, Wyeast 4021, White Labs WLP715

White Labs and Wyeast Laboratories supply their yeast strains as liquid cultures, while the other vendors supply their products as dried yeast.

Fermentis Yeasts

Vendor Code	Common Name	Temperature Range	Alcohol Tolerance	Comments
S101	Saint Georges	From 46°F (8°C)	Good	Medium nitrogen requirements and high ester production; develops fruit and flower aromas.
CK S102		From 46°F (8°C)	14.5%	Strong nitrogen requirement; intensifies aromas of white wines and has high production of esters; at 50–54°F (10–12°C) has tropical taste like mango and pineapple, at 61–64°F (16–19°C) has citrus taste like grapefruit.
BC S103		50–95°F (10–35°C)	18%	Low nitrogen requirements and low production of higher alcohols; useful for restarting stuck ferments.

Lallemand Yeasts

Vendor Code	Common Name	Temperature Range	Alcohol Tolerance	Comments
Enoferm Assmanshausen		68–86°F (20–30°C)	15%	Medium nitrogen requirement; enhances spicy notes (clove, nutmeg) and fruit characteristics.
ICV-K1 (V 1116)		50–95°F (10–35°C)	18%	Medium requirement for nitrogen and high requirement for oxygen; when used at cool temperatures (below 61°F, 16°C) with proper nutrients, produces floral esters.
EC 1118	Prise de Mousse	50–86°F (10–30°C), optimum is 59–77°F (15–25°C)	18%	Original Prise de Mousse strain; champagne strain with low nitrogen requirement and low oxygen requirement; tolerates wide range of pH during fermentation; under low nutrient conditions will produce considerable SO_2.
71B-1122	Narbonne	59–86°F (15–30°C)	14%	Low nitrogen requirement; metabolizes 20–40% of malic acid in must and can produce significant esters; reduction of malic acid can be beneficial in melomels made from fruits high in malic acid.
ICV D47	Côtes du Rhône	59–86°F (15–30°C), best at 68°F (20°C)	14%	Low nitrogen requirement and average requirement for oxygen; lees produce ripe, spicy aromas of tropical fruit and citrus; accentuates fruit characteristics.
RC 212	Bourgorouge	59–86°F (18–30°C)	16%	Medium nitrogen requirement; known for producing red wines with good structure, ripe cherry, and bright fruit and spicy characteristics.

Lallemand provides many strains of yeast, but many are focused on commercial users and are not available in packages smaller than 500 grams.

Red Star Yeasts

Vendor Code	Temperature Range	Alcohol Tolerance	Comments
Montrachet	59–86°F (15–30°C)	13%	Considered neutral yeast. (UC-Davis strain 522)
Pasteur Champagne	59–86°F (15–30°C)	13–15%	Considered neutral and doesn't produce much yeast-derived character. (UC-Davis strain 595)
Côte des Blancs	64–86°F (18–30°C)	12–14%	Also known as Epernay II; slow fermenter that tends not to ferment to dryness. (UC-Davis strain 750)
Premier Cuvée	45–95°F (7-35°C)	18%	Frequently used to restart stuck fermentations because of high alcohol tolerance; said to be Prise de Mousse strain. (UC-Davis strain 796)
Pasteur Red	59–86°F (18–30°C)	16%	Classic red wine strain. (UC-Davis strain 904)

Vintner's Harvest Yeasts

Vendor Code	Temperature Range	Alcohol Tolerance	Comments
AW4	68–77°F (20–25°C)	14.5%	Produces fragrant, spicy aromas; associated with Gewürztraminer wines.
CL23	46–75°F (7–24°C)	18%	Fairly neutral white wine yeast; will remove color and fruity characteristics. (Saccharomyces Bayanus)
CR51	72–86°F (22–30°C)	13.5%	Will enhance berry fruit characteristics.
CY17	72–78°F (22–30°C)	15%	Requires constant fermentation temperature, dropping temperature partway through fermentation will arrest fermentation; metabisulfite and potassium sorbate required to prevent renewed fermentation; slow fermenter; delicate strain; pH should be above 3.2 and SO_2 levels below 50 ppm; start fermentation warm.
MA23	64–80°F (18–27°C)	14%	Will metabolize 30–35% of malic acid in must, good for melomels made from high acid fruits; produces esters and fusels; may require late addition of oxygen to complete fermentation.
SN9	As low as 50°F (10°C)	18%	A robust strain that is tolerant of high SO_2 levels, incorrect temperatures, and poor pH control. It is good for restarting stuck fermentations. Saccharomyces Bayanus.

White Labs Yeasts

Vendor Code	Common Name	Temperature Range	Alcohol Tolerance	Comments
WLP707	California Pinot Noir	To over 70°F (21°C)	17%	Produces fruit and complex aromas.
WLP715	Champagne	70–75°F (21–24°C)	17%	Champagne yeasts are considered neutral and don't produce much yeast-derived character in the mead.
WLP718	Avize	60–90°F (16–32°C)	15%	Used for complexity in white wines.
WLP720	Sweet Mead/Wine	70–75°F (21–24°C)	15%	Will leave some residual sugar in the mead.
WLP727	Steinberg-Geisenheim	50–90°F (10–32°C)	14%	Produces a high amount of fruity esters.
WLP730	Chardonnay	50–90°F (10–32°C)	14%	A low ester producer.
WLP735	French White	60–90°F (16-32°C)	16%	A classic white wine strain.
WLP740	Merlot Red	60–90°F (15.6–32° C)	18%	Has a neutral profile with low production of fusel alcohols.
WLP749	Assmanshausen	50–90° F (10–32°C)	16%	Produces the German red wine spicy, fruit characteristics.
WLP750	French Red	60–90°F (15.6–32°C)	17%	Classic Bordeaux strain, tolerates lower fermentation temperatures, with rich and smooth profile.
WLP760	Cabernet Red	60–90°F (16–32°C)	16%	For full-bodied red wines.
WLP770	Suremain Burgundy	60–90°F (16–32°C)	16%	Has a high nutrient requirement and emphasizes fruit characteristics.
WLP775	English Cider	68–75°F (20–24°C)	Medium-high	Classic cider strain ferments dry but retains apple flavor; great for cysers.

Wyeast Yeasts

Vendor Code	Common Name	Temperature Range	Alcohol Tolerance	Comments
4021	Pasteur Champagne	45–75°F (7–24°C)	17%	Ferments crisp and dry.
4028	Chateau Red	50–95°F (10–35°C)	14%	Typically for reds and whites that mature quickly with Beaujolais fruitiness.
4184	Sweet Mead/Wine	65–75°F (18–24°C)	11%	Leaves 2–3% residual sugar, produces a rich fruity profile.
4242	Chablis	55–75°F (12–24°C)	12–13%	Extremely fruity profile, bready aroma with vanilla notes.
4244	Chianti	55–75°F (13–24°C)	14%	Rich, big, and bold profile, soft fruit character.
4267	Bordeaux	60–90°F (16–32°C)	14%	Produces a distinctive intense berry, graham-cracker aroma; jammy, rich, smooth complex profile; slightly vinous.
4632	Dry Mead	55–75°F (13–24°C)	18%	
4767	Port	60–90°F (16–32°C)	14%	Mild toast and vanilla, mild fruit, very dry finish.
4783	Rudesheimer	55–75°F (13–24°C)	14%	Produces a distinctive Riesling character; rich, creamy, fruity profile.
4946	Zinfandel	60–85°F (16–29°C)	18%	Dominating, strong fermentation characteristic.

NONTRADITIONAL YEASTS

Yeast belongs to the genus of organisms called *Saccharomyces*. Most mead, wine, and beer yeasts are either *S. cerevisiae* or *S. bayanus*. The craft brewing world has shown a lot of interest in using *Brettanomyces (Brett)* either in combination with *Saccharomyces* or in a pure *Brett* fermentation.

The main yeast suppliers offer a handful of strains of *Brett*, but the detailed sensory profiles, nutrient needs, and fermentation performance are not nearly as well researched and documented as for the common *Saccharomyces* strains. Most of the descriptions are going to be focused on beer, not mead, fermentations.

Pure *Brett* fermentations tend to differ from fermentations that have both *Saccharomyces* and *Brett*. The results of pure *Brett* fermentations seem similar to *Saccharomyces* fermentations, though with a significant ester level that tends toward tropical fruit characteristics. Mixed fermentations can carry complex characteristics such as those found in some farmhouse-style ales, including leatherlike, sour, fruity, and so on. Pure *Brett* fermentations generally process as quickly as regular *Saccharomyces* fermentations, but mixed fermentations may take a long time to fully develop the end characteristics. Most *Brett* strains appear to be alcohol tolerant in ABVs of at least the low teens, although that can be influenced by fermentation characteristics (oxygen, nutrients, and temperature).

Brett is available only as a liquid, meaning you may need to grow the culture in a starter to get enough for your batch. *Brett* responds just like regular yeast in a starter environment. I grow it in a flask on a stir plate.

One caution with *Brett* fermentations: if you are bottling your mead, *Brett* tends to ferment nearly all the sugars in the must. Unless you start with a really huge original gravity, you should assume the *Brett* will eventually take the mead down to the 1.004–1.008 range or lower, and the rate of fermentation may slow significantly near the end. If you bottle too soon, you may end up with exploding bottles.

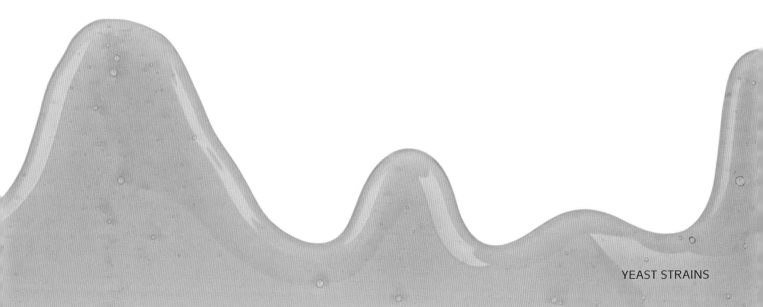

5 THE BASIC PROCESS

MOST MEAD MUSTS HAVE A HIGH SUGAR LEVEL THAT STRESSES THE YEAST CELLS, and most honeys lack essential nutrients for yeasts. In a process called staggered nutrient addition (SNA), nutrients are added during the first part of the fermentation as the yeast grows. If all the nutrients were added from the start, your mead would have a high population of yeast cells with relatively low protein content. Fewer total cells are grown with staged addition, but the cells are healthier, have higher protein content, and are not as vulnerable to alcohol toxicity (when yeast cells slow down or stop fermenting as the alcohol level goes up). Further, undesirable microorganisms (wild yeast, bacteria) may consume all of the nutrients if you add them in the beginning, microorganisms that may affect the mead by producing improper aromas and flavors.

Unhealthy yeast cells tend to produce more higher alcohols than healthy yeast. Some call these higher alcohols fusels, fusel alcohols, or fusel oils. They are generally perceived as hot, unpleasant side effects of fermentations. Fusels—or byproducts from the amino acid production necessary for building proteins—are one reason some people think meads need to age for a long time before becoming drinkable. Ensuring that the yeast cells receive enough nutrients minimizes the production of fusels. Fusels, however, can also be converted into flavor-active compounds called esters by combining them with organic acids.

Meadmaking calls for periodic stirring of the fermentation, which has several advantages. First, it helps remove carbon dioxide (CO_2) from the solution. (CO_2 can be toxic to the yeast.) Second, it periodically introduces oxygen, contributing to yeast health. Adding nutrients helps, but yeasts also need oxygen to produce the proteins, sterols, and fatty acids essential for proper fermentation.

Mead recipes frequently call for boiling the must and then chilling it before pitching the yeast, and they typically direct meadmakers to skim the scum (coagulated proteins) from the surface during the boil. Many claim that boiling the must creates a clear mead at the end of fermentation. However, honey and many fruits have delicate flavors and aromas that boiling may change or eliminate. I skip the boil and keep the aromatics and delicate flavors in my mead. The topic of boiling is hotly debated, but none of the good meadmakers I know boil their must. Instead, they achieve a clear mead with elapsed time or other techniques (covered later in this book).

Recipes that call for the addition of acids during must creation typically push the pH too far into the acidic (low pH) range for a robust fermentation by the yeast. If the pH of the finished mead needs more acid for balance, I adjust the balance post-fermentation.

RECORDKEEPING

Good meadmakers keep detailed records of their production for several reasons. First, if you make a mead that you really like and want to make again, you will have the information needed to reproduce it. Second, if you taste one of your meads and find something in its characteristics you want to change, records can help you determine where changes might impact the characteristics. Also, if you enter your mead in a competition, records can help you identify changes in your process to address issues noted by the judges.

Detailed records include more than just a list of ingredients used. You want to keep notes on everything you did: all the times you stirred the mead, the times of nutrient additions, the intermediate temperatures and specific gravities, and even your perceptions of the mead during its development and aging. As you note the aging conditions of the mead—for example, if you moved the finished mead from room temperature storage to the refrigerator—record each transition. See page 153 for a completed log page.

SANITATION

For fermented products like mead, sanitation of all equipment that comes in contact with the ingredients or with the end product is extremely important. Before you can sanitize anything, it needs to be clean, and most sanitizers are not cleansers. Standard kitchen detergents aren't great for cleaning brewing equipment, because these detergents tend to leave residues that must be rinsed extensively. Lightly soiled durable items can be scrubbed with a soft cloth or sponge. Soak heavily soiled items in a brewery cleaner such as Five Star's PBW, then gently scrub them with a cloth or sponge. Be sure to follow the instructions when mixing up these cleaners. Once everything is clean, it is time for sanitation.

Batch Name:				
Mead Type:				
Description:				
Date:	Target Batch Size:	Target OG:		Target FG:
Water source and treatment:				

INGREDIENTS

Amount	Ingredient	When Added

Actual SG:	Actual Volume:

NUTRIENT MIXTURE

Amount	Nutrient Name	

STAGGERED NUTRIENT ADDITIONS

Amount	When Added	Other Notes	

YEAST

Rehydration

Yeast Strain:	Yeast Amount Used:	
Rehydration Nutrient:	Rehydration Nutrient Amount:	
Rehydration Water Source:	Rehydration Water Amount:	
Rehydration Temperature:		
Rehydration Start Time:	Rehydration End Time:	

Yeast Starter

Starter Size:	Starter Source:	

COMBINING YEAST WITH MUST

Yeast Temperature:	Must Temperature:	
Temperature Difference:	Atempering Steps:	
Atemper Step Number:	When:	
Atemper Step Number:	When:	
Atemper Step Number:	When:	

MEASUREMENTS

When	SG	Temperature	Other Notes	

ADJUSTMENTS

When	Amount	What Used	Other Comments	

SANITIZING

1. Mix up the sanitizing solution with 0.5 ounces (15 milliliters) of the Star San concentrate and 2.5 gallons (9.46 liters) of tap water in a large bucket with a cover. If your house has a water softener, use water that went through the softener. The solution will stay useable for a long time if made with "soft" water, and not nearly as long if made with the "hard" water. The sanitizer solution is effective after just a couple of minutes of contact time. You don't need to completely fill containers to sanitize them—completely wetting the inside with the solution is sufficient. Don't rinse after sanitizing, even if there is foam. The foam will not cause any problems in your mead. You also don't need to mix up a new batch of sanitizer solution every time—you can store it in the bucket with the cover on it to keep out dust and lint.

2. Put a few cups of the sanitizer solution into a 5-gallon (19-liter) container with a lid. Slosh the solution around to wet the entire inside of the container and then dump the residual sanitizer solution back into the sanitizer bucket. (Be sure to wet the entire inside of the container's lid with the solution as well.) Place the thermometer into the bucket of sanitizer solution and wet the entire surface.

3. After running 5 gallons (19-liters) of tap water into the sanitized container (if your house has a water softener, use unsoftened water), use a clean dry spoon against the inside of the measuring cup to crush one Campden tablet and then dump it into the sanitized container of water. Stir to dissolve.

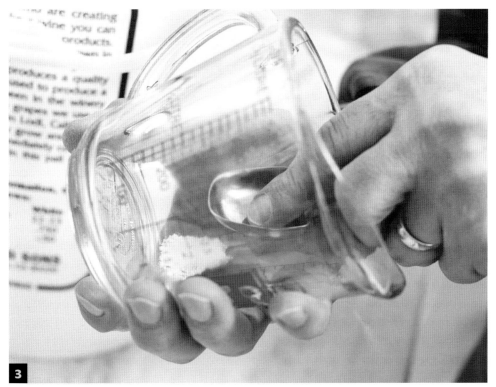

4. Place the thermometer in the container of water; we want room-temperature water in the 65–75°F (18–24°C) range. If the water is too hot or too cold, place the lid on the water container and just let it stand until the temperature is in range. Return the thermometer to the sanitizer solution.

5. Pour a few cups (1 liter) of the sanitizer solution into the large plastic fermenter and swirl it around to make sure it contacts the entire inside surface. Pour the residual sanitizer out of the large fermenter and back into the bucket of sanitizer solution. Be sure to wet the inside of the fermenter's lid with sanitizer solution.

6. Place the large spoon, the kitchen spatula, the measuring cup, and the hydrometer in the bucket of sanitizer one by one and splash sanitizer over each, being sure to sanitize all surfaces, including the handles.

Some references suggest using household bleach as a sanitizer, but I don't recommend using bleach. Items need to be rinsed after bleaching, which risks reintroducing wild yeast and bacteria. Improper rinsing of bleach will result in chlorophenols, a family of unpleasant-smelling and -tasting chemicals. Many winemaking references suggest using metabisulfites, which will work but require long contact times and can be touchy. I avoid sulfites.

Of the several types of modern sanitizers on the market today, I prefer to use Five Star's Star San—a fast-acting, acid-based sanitizer that does not require rinsing. In fact, *do not rinse it*, or you risk undoing the sanitation. Even the residual foam should be left on the sanitized object; the extremely small amount of Star San left over after draining will not impact the aroma or flavor of your mead.

Star San concentrate is typically sold in plastic containers with a built-in measuring device. I like to mix up 2.5 gallons (9.5 liters) of sanitizer in a bucket and keep it on hand, storing it in a covered bucket to keep the dust out. Always follow the package instructions for the amount of concentrate to use. Star San calls for 1 ounce (30 milliliters) of concentrate to make five gallons (19 liters) of sanitizing solution, or 0.5 ounces (15 milliliters) Star San for 2.5 gallons (9.5 liters) solution. If your house has a water softener (meaning you likely have fairly hard water to begin with), you want to mix up the Star San using water that came through the water softener. The mixed solution is effective as long as it isn't cloudy, generally as long as the pH is 3.0 or lower.

Sanitation requires 1–2 minutes of contact time; the object needs to be totally wet but does not need to be immersed or filled with the solution. I like to keep a small household spray bottle full of Star San sanitizer solution around to spray the airlock and stopper of a carboy before removing it, and I can spray the inside of a large fermenter with sanitizer more easily than I can slosh the solution around to wet the inside.

WATER

Generally, if your water tastes OK, you can use it to make mead, but I don't recommend distilled or deionized water. In general, relatively hard water is desirable for meadmaking because it helps buffer the mead from getting too acidic during fermentation. The buffering action of hard water typically comes from the carbonates that resist lowering the pH of the water. During fermentation the pH of the fermenting beverage will drop (become more acidic), but if it drops too far, the yeast will have problems finishing the fermentation.

In the United States, virtually all municipal water supplies are treated with chlorine or chloramine to kill pathogenic microbes and protect public health. Chlorine is fairly easy to smell, but chloramine may not have a strong odor. Many jurisdictions that were using chlorine are moving to chloramine for its stability. (It's harder to remove.) You do not want chlorine or chloramine in the water you use to make mead, because either can form chemical compounds known as chlorophenols, which generally exhibit plasticlike, medicinal, electrical fire, and other unpleasant characteristics. The human detection threshold for many chlorophenols is extremely low, meaning it doesn't take much for them to be noticeable in your mead.

An activated charcoal filter like this under-sink variety will remove volatile organic compounds as well as chlorine and chloramine from your water. It will not remove dissolved inorganic substances (nor will it remove hardness), but it will remove some unpleasant aromas and flavors.

To eliminate the risk of chlorophenols from your water, you need to remove the chlorine or chloramines. You can remove chlorine (but not chloramine) from water just by boiling it for a few minutes. Both chlorine and chloramine can be removed by adding potassium or sodium metabisulfite. Dissolving a Campden tablet provides the proper amount of metabisulfite to remove all the chlorine and/or chloramine in up to 20 gallons (76 liters) of water. Let the water set for 10–15 minutes for the reaction to complete. The slight residual sulfites will not harm the fermentation and will typically be eliminated by the end.

You can also treat your water with an activated charcoal filter, which will remove volatile organic compounds as well as chlorine and chloramine. The filter does not remove dissolved inorganic substances from the water (nor will it remove hardness), but it will remove unpleasant aromas and flavors in some water sources. I use an under-sink type of household filter housing set up with garden hose–style fittings on the input side and a granular carbon (activated charcoal) cartridge inside the housing.

Finally, while the procedures described above will eliminate chlorine or chloramine as a source of chlorophenols in your mead, beware that undesirable phenols can still make their way into your mead. For example, failure to properly sanitize your equipment could result in contamination by wild yeasts, and some wild yeast strains can produce medicinal, plasticlike, smoky, and other phenols. Improper sanitation chemicals can also contribute to chlorophenols as can use of nonfood-grade plastics.

MEASURING HONEY

Honey leaves strands of sticky sweetness everywhere when you pour it, and it is nearly always difficult to get out of a container. My meadmaking approach doesn't depend on getting a precise amount of honey into the fermenter, but I still want to get close to the planned amount so that I come close to the planned batch size.

I place a sanitized plastic fermenter on my scale and tare the scale (set it to zero). Then I start pouring the honey into the fermenter and stop when I get close to the desired amount, using a sanitized spatula to get all the threads of honey. If I've used all the honey in the container, I get the small amount still coating the inside later when I start adding liquid to make the mead.

If you buy honey in bulk, typically in 5-gallon (19-liter) buckets, try to get a bucket lid with a spout. The typical spout has a screw-top cover that is fairly easy to unscrew if you don't let it get stuck on the honey left over from the last time you used it. Alternatively, you can use a large sanitized measuring cup or pitcher to scoop honey out of the bucket.

It is fine to use crystallized honey when making mead, though it can be a bit harder to work with. You can set the covered jug in a bucket of hot water to soften the honey, but that may not be sufficient to soften the whole contents. I sometimes have to resort to using a sharp knife to cut a large hole in the top of the jug to extract the honey. You can place the container of crystallized honey in an oven set for approximately 125–150°F (52–66°C) for a couple of hours to soften the honey and make it easier to work with. Crystallized honey is usually easier to remove from a bucket than from a jug, but beware that stirring it may bend your large spoon if the honey is really crystallized.

A good rule of thumb for measuring honey is that 1 gallon (3.79 liters) of honey weighs approximately 12 pounds (5.44 kilograms), with slight variations due to the moisture content of the honey.

MIXING THE MUST

Once you have the honey and some water in the fermenter, you need to get them mixed together. I find once I have roughly twice the volume of honey as water (or other liquid) in the fermenter, it becomes easier to get the honey dissolved. You can use a large spoon to do the mixing, but it can be tiring, especially if your honey has started to crystallize. I prefer to use a stainless steel wand made for degassing wine. The wand has a couple of foldout paddles on one end, and the other end goes into an electric drill. I sanitize the wand in my Star San solution and then place it in the fermenter. Once the top is chucked into the drill, I start to stir slowly. Don't get carried away with the drill speed, or you will likely splash the sticky solution everywhere. The aggressive stirring needed to get all the honey dissolved has the secondary benefit of oxygenating the must.

FRUIT IN PRIMARY

There are two schools of thought on adding fruit to mead: one that suggests adding the fruit after primary fermentation has slowed significantly (fruit in secondary) and one that calls for putting the fruit in the primary fermenter right from the start (fruit in primary).

Those who advocate the fruit in secondary approach assert that the fruit's fragile characteristics will be better maintained when added after the vigorous fermentation has stopped producing large amounts of carbon dioxide. However, the fruit has to sit in the nearly finished fermentation for weeks or even months to extract all the characteristics of the fruit. Also, the fruit may contribute enough sugar to the mead to restart fermentation; or if the initial fermentation was stopped by the yeast reaching its alcohol limit, the addition of fruit (largely made up of water) may reduce the alcohol level and allow fermentation to start again. As a final drawback to this method, the mead may require significant aging to meld the fruit and honey.

In the fruit in primary approach, the fruit provides nutrients to the yeast and melds with the developing mead and alcohol from day one. You eliminate the risk of restarting fermentation weeks into the production cycle, and I think the fruit character is more pleasant if fermented with the honey right from the start. In addition, putting the fruit in the primary is going to help break down the fruit. Exposing the fruit to primary fermentation results in a different ester profile than you would get by adding the fruit later in the fermentation. (Esters are the chemicals that we perceive as fruity.)

I always add fruits to my meads during the primary fermentation right when I add the yeast, which means the fruit, juice, or fruit concentrates all go in the primary fermenter. It's easier to work with the whole fruit or chunks of fruit in a container with a removable lid than it is in a carboy. For some fruits, I prefer to put the fruit into a large mesh bag that then goes into the fermenter; the bag makes it easier to remove the fruit later. I don't use chemical sanitizers for the fabric bags, though. I put a bag in a small pot of water and boil it for a few minutes to sanitize it.

HOW MUCH YEAST DO I NEED?

The calculator under "Yeast Tools" at www.mrmalty.com can help you determine how much yeast you will need for your mead. Primarily devoted to beer brewing, the calculator allows you to choose ale, lager, and hybrid under "Fermentation Types." I use the calculator in the ale mode; to me, mead and wine yeasts are more like ale yeasts than the other choices. The tool takes as inputs the batch size and the original gravity of the must. Then you select the type of yeast you are using—liquid or dried. The tool tells you how many grams of dried yeast to you need. (The packets are typically labeled in grams.) Liquid yeast has more options, depending on how you plan to handle the yeast. The tool will tell you how many packages of liquid yeast and how big of a starter you will need as a function of how you process the starter. You can find further details on rehydration of dried yeast and using a starter for liquid yeast in Chapter 4.

PITCHING THE YEAST INTO THE MUST

With either rehydrated dried yeast or the results of a starter, you don't want to thermally shock the yeast when you pitch it into the must. That means you don't want the temperature of the yeast to encounter more than an 18°F (10°C) temperature drop. Starters grown at room temperature and pitched into a must at room temperature don't generally have problems, but rehydrated dried yeast has an average temperature of around 100°F (38°C) at the end of the rehydration period, and the must is going to be much cooler.

For each 18°F (10°C) difference in temperature between the yeast mixture and the must, you will need to perform an atemperation step that allows the yeast to adjust to the must temperature slowly. Record both the must temperature and the yeast mixture temperature in your log, noting the difference. If atemperation is required, slowly add a small amount of must to the yeast mixture, over about 5 minutes, stirring gently. Make sure not to lower the temperature of the yeast mixture by more than 18°F (10°C). Let the mixture atemper for 15–20 minutes. If the temperature of the yeast mixture is still more than 18°F (10°C) above the must temperature, repeat the process. Generally, doubling the volume of the yeast suspension by adding must will put the new temperature at the midpoint between the must temperature and the rehydration temperature.

STAGGERED NUTRIENT ADDITION

The basic approach of staggered nutrient addition detailed here works with typical must formulations.

Yeast, a single-cell living organism, creates much of what it needs from the basic building blocks in its surroundings, but sometimes this process releases undesirable characteristics into the fermentation. And if some of the basics are missing, the resulting fermentation can be problematic. These problems can be avoided by giving the yeast an easy path to what it wants.

Honey is a pretty minimal environment low in free amino nitrogen (FAN) and many other trace elements needed for fermentation. You must add nitrogen to help the yeast synthesize proteins and reproduce to sufficient numbers to complete the fermentation properly. Adding diammonium phosphate (DAP) and Fermaid K provides the nitrogen and other elements and vitamins the yeast needs.

Staggered nutrient additions keep the yeast happily growing and working during the first days of fermentation, which results in better mead. For the typical 5-gallon batch of mead, use 4 grams Fermaid K (approximately $1/2$ teaspoon plus $1/3$ teaspoon, 0.14 ounce by weight) and 8 grams DAP (approximately 1 teaspoon plus $2/3$ teaspoons, 0.28 ounce by weight) mixed together. I like to measure the nutrients into a resealable plastic bag at the start of the batch and keep the bag next to the fermenter to make sure that I get all the nutrients into the batch. Determining the perfect amounts would require detailed chemical analysis of the must as well as a comprehensive understanding of the yeast strain's nutrient needs. If your batch size is not 5 gallons, adjust the amounts accordingly. If the batch is a fraction of a gallon bigger or smaller, I don't adjust the quantities, since the amounts are just nominal values to start with. If you do not have a scale capable of measuring fractions of a gram, my measurements show that an average weight of 1 teaspoon of DAP is 5 grams, and the weight of 1 teaspoon of Fermaid K is 4.77 grams.

The additions are timed according to a typical fermentation performance by the yeast. A warm fermentation temperature can speed up fermentation, and a cool fermentation temperature can slow down fermentation. The first three doses give the yeast nutrients while it is still in the exponential growth phase of the fermentation, and the addition at 30 percent completion gives the yeast a final nutrient boost as it enters the stationary phase of the fermentation.

Staggered Nutrient Addition

Amount	When
2 grams (approximately ¾ teaspoon)	At initial mixing of must
2 grams (approximately ¾ teaspoon)	After 48 hours
2 grams (approximately ¾ teaspoon)	After 96 hours
2 grams (approximately ¾ teaspoon)	After SG has dropped to just 30% of the planned value

To estimate when you have reached 30 percent of the target final gravity (FG), you need the starting gravity (SG) and the target final gravity (FG) for the batch.

Estimating 30% of Target FG Working in Degrees Fahrenheit

$$30\% \: SG = 1 + \left((SG - 1.000) - \left(\left((SG - 1.000) - (FG - 1.000) \right) \right) \times 0.3 \right)$$

Things look much simpler if you work in degrees Brix or Plato.

Estimating 30% of Target FG Working in Degrees Brix or Plato

30% SG = SG - ((SG - FG) x 0.3)

When it is time to add the nutrients, beware that dry powders are nucleation sites for all the carbon dioxide dissolved in the fermenting mead. Be sure to wait to add the nutrients until after you have completed one of your periodic stirrings of the mead, or you will likely create a gusher of fermenting mead—probably not as impressive as the Mentos and Diet Coke eruption from the Mythbusters TV show, but it can still be messy to clean up.

PERIODIC STIRRING

You must stir the must several times a day for the first eight days of the fermentation. The fermenting mead is saturated with dissolved carbon dioxide, which can become toxic to the yeast and result in reduced fermentation performance, and stirring releases it. Stirring can prevent carbon dioxide from causing a higher final gravity and lower attenuation (the difference between the starting gravity and the final gravity; higher starting gravity increases the potential for more alcohol). The first few seconds of stirring usually don't cause a lot of bubbles, but then the volume of bubbles starts to increase rapidly. Start slowly and control your stirring rate so that you don't end up with foam going over the top of your fermenter.

You can use a large spoon, but be prepared for a fair amount of stirring until no new bubbles are being released by the action. I typically use a stainless steel wand made for degassing wine that fits into an electric drill—the same wand I use for initially mixing the must. Using a variable-speed drill, I start out slow and control the speed to keep the volume of foam under control.

For meads with fruit added to the fermenter, you must periodically punch the cap (the floating mass of fruit) down into the must to keep it cool. The active yeast in the cap that is drying out may get warmer than the planned fermentation temperature and will contribute unpleasant flavors. Keeping the fruit wet in the must will also help extract the flavors and aromas. When I have the fruit in a large mesh bag, I remove the whole bag of fruit and place it in a sanitized bucket while stirring the mead. After the stirring is finished, I put the bag back in the fermenter and use a large spoon to push it down in the must and saturate it.

In the commercial brewing and winemaking world, there are studies of the impact of carbon dioxide pressure on the production of yeast byproducts such as esters and fusels. Commercial operations typically have sealed fermenters that can retain positive carbon dioxide pressure, but home meadmakers rarely have fermenters that can hold pressure and/or that are deep enough for the dissolved carbon dioxide pressures to have significant impact on the secondary characteristics produced by the yeast. (I don't consider a carboy with an airlock to be a pressurized vessel.)

FERMENTATION

Much of the homebrewing literature tends to confuse people with the term *secondary fermentation*. A true secondary fermentation involves the addition of more fermentable sugar and perhaps even new yeast, a process that is still used for some carbonated, bottle-conditioned beverages. There is no secondary fermentation in the production of most commercial beer, wine, and mead, but rather a transfer of the fermenting beverage into a secondary container partway through the fermentation process.

INITIAL FERMENTATION

The initial fermentation takes place in a plastic vessel, either a food-grade bucket or a purpose-made plastic fermenter with a removable lid. The removable lid makes stirring easy, to get the honey initially dissolved, and it makes the management of fruit much easier. Finally, plastic tends to be much less fragile than glass. However, during the very active initial stage of fermentation, the yeast will consume all the oxygen that gets into the must, but these large containers with removable lids also let too much oxygen into the developing mead once the fermentation has slowed down, which requires close monitoring so the must is moved to the carboy before oxygenation occurs.

FINISHING FERMENTATION

Fermentation is finished in a carboy, either glass or plastic. After the fermentation has slowed, the nutrients have been added, and the equipment has been sanitized, transfer the mead via a siphon from the initial (primary) fermenter into the carboy. Any fruit added to the mead is left behind at this point.

I try to use a carboy as close to the batch size as possible to minimize headspace (the air space left at the top of the carboy after siphoning in the mead). Too much headspace can result in oxidation of the mead as the fermentation slows down and quits generating carbon dioxide. Depending on the size of the batch and the sizes of carboys I have available, I may transfer the mead into several carboys. I don't normally leave my meads in a carboy for more than a few months, but the longer the time in the carboy, the more important it becomes to minimize headspace. Since I have a kegging system, I can transfer the mead from the carboy into one or more kegs and eliminate headspace issues once fermentation has finished. I use nitrogen to maintain positive pressure in the keg to ensure the lid stays sealed. Some winemakers sanitize a bunch of glass marbles (frequently sold in craft stores for decorating purposes), then gently drop enough marbles into the carboy to fill all the headspace. You need to be careful when dropping glass marbles into glass carboys, however; I would be more comfortable doing this with a plastic carboy.

The fermentation will finish in the carboy, and the mead may begin to clarify as the yeast cells start to drop out of suspension (one sign that the fermentation is ending). The process of the yeast dropping to the bottom is called flocculation, but some yeast strains do not flocculate as well as others. Another way to determine if the fermentation has ended is to actually measure the specific gravity over several days by extracting some with a sanitized wine thief (a long tube inserted through the small neck of the carboy to extract a sample). Lower a typical wine thief into the carboy, place a finger over the hole at the top to keep the liquid inside while you remove it, then remove the finger over the hole and allow the mead to drain into the hydrometer sample jar. Depending on the size of the sample jar and the size of the thief, you may need to repeat the process several times. Record the specific gravity in your log. Repeat the process after a few days, and if the specific gravity hasn't changed, fermentation is done, and you can move on to finishing your mead.

STEP-BY-STEP INSTRUCTIONS FOR MAKING YOUR FIRST MEAD

Without worrying about why we do any of these steps, let's walk through the process of making a batch of straight mead, (a mead made with just honey, water, and yeast). Using these steps to create a still, semisweet mead will help you refine your techniques and then adjust for your tastes. The key is to follow the steps precisely.

This recipe uses orange blossom honey—one of the general-purpose honeys most readily available to meadmakers. If you cannot obtain orange blossom honey, go with clover honey, but I advise against substituting wildflower honey.

The plan is to make approximately 5 gallons (19 liters) of sack-strength mead with a starting specific gravity around 1.115 and a finishing specific gravity around 1.010. If you miss on the final gravity, you will most likely come in high, so you will still get a mead— just a little sweeter one than you intended.

If you have made mead before, you might find the description of the steps overly detailed. As you gain experience, you can customize the process for your equipment and brewing style.

Ingredients

Approximately 14 pounds (6.35 kilograms) orange blossom honey

5 grams Go-Ferm (approximately 1½ teaspoons)

4 grams Fermaid K (approximately ½ teaspoon plus ⅓ teaspoon, 0.14 ounce by weight)

8 grams diammonium phosphate (approximately 1⅔ teaspoons, 0.28 ounce by weight)

1 packet (4 grams) Lallemand 71B-1122 (Narbonne) yeast

1 Campden tablet

1 packet Super-Kleer K.C. Finings

1 container Star San sanitizer concentrate

Basic Size-Specific Equipment

The basic equipment is unique to the batch size the equipment can make, but the rest of the equipment is common to all batch sizes.

One-Gallon Batch

The 1-gallon (3.79liter) system will likely yield 8–10 finished 12-ounce (330–375 milliliter) bottles of mead. The system doesn't take much room to store, individual batches don't cost a lot, and you can experiment with recipes you aren't sure will work well. Plus, there are no heavy full carboys to move around when it comes time to transfer the mead. However, if you end up really liking the mead, you are going to wish you had made more of it.

The size-specific equipment includes:

- 2 glass 1-gallon (3.8–4 liter) jugs
- Stoppers and airlocks that fit the jugs
- A 2-gallon (7.5–8 liter) or larger plastic fermenting bucket with lid and airlock

Three-Gallon Batch

The 3-gallon (11–12 liter) system is a little more versatile than the 1-gallon (3.79-liter) setup. It should yield 24–30 finished 12-ounce (330–375 milliliter) bottles of mead, but the pieces are a little bigger and a little more expensive than the 1-gallon setup. The full carboys still aren't overly heavy; in the range of 35 pounds (15–16 kilograms).

The size-specific equipment includes:

- 2 3-gallon (11–12 liter) carboys
- Stoppers and airlocks that fit the carboys
- A 6-gallon (22–23 liter) or larger plastic fermenter with lid and airlock

Five-Gallon Batch

The 5-gallon (19-liter) system fits most mead recipes you will find elsewhere, and the recipe development chapter (Chapter 10) will show you how to scale them to the size you want. The full carboys will weigh about 50 pounds (22–23 kilograms)—a little bigger to store. If you are already making beer, you probably have equipment this size.

The size-specific equipment includes:

- 2 5-gallon (19-liter) glass carboys or 1 5-gallon (19-liter) and 1 6-gallon (23-liter) carboy
- Stoppers and airlocks to fit the carboys
- A 10-gallon (38-liter) or larger open-top plastic fermenter with lid

Most of my fermenters have volume markings on them: I used a paint marker (a felt-tip pen that writes with paint) to write directly on some; on some I wrote with a paint felt-tip pen on a piece of vinyl tape from a label maker; and on plastic fermenters I used a regular felt-tip marker. I added a gallon of water and then marked the fermenter appropriately. If you prefer to use metric volume, mark it every couple of liters.

Some basic equipment needed for meadmaking includes: a large stainless steel mixing spoon, hydrometer test container, spatula, thermometer, hydrometer, one or two small spoons, autosiphon, stirring and bottling wands, and a kitchen scale (the old-school dial type works well for measuring honey).

Common Equipment

- Large food-grade plastic fermenter with cover—at least 6 gallons (23 liters)
- 5-gallon (19-liter) bucket and lid for storing mixed sanitizer
- 5-gallon (19-liter) container with lid for treating water
- Large stainless steel mixing spoon
- Kitchen spatula
- Large measuring cup (glass or hard plastic)
- Set of kitchen measuring spoons
- Hydrometer and test container
- Thermometer (floating)
- 5-gallon (19-liter) carboy with stopper and airlock
- Autosiphon (There are small ones for 1-gallon batches, but if you think you are going to eventually make bigger batches, go for the standard-size one)
- 5 feet (1.5 meters) of $5/16$-inch (inside diameter) clear plastic racking hose
- Bottling wand
- Small resealable plastic bag
- Small (8–16 ounce, 0.25–0.5 liter) glass or plastic measuring cup to rehydrate the yeast
- Small spoon for stirring the yeast during rehydration
- Plastic cling wrap to cover the yeast during rehydration
- Scissors
- Approximately 2 cases (24 bottles per case) of 12-ounce (350–375 milliliter) beer bottles
- Bottle capper
- Bottle caps for the bottles
- A plastic bottle filler
- Water glasses

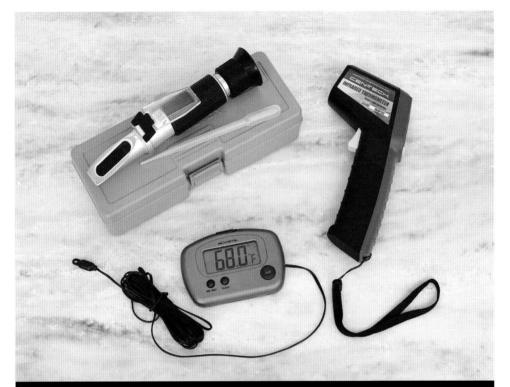

Left: Who doesn't like gadgets? An infrared thermometer and refractometer (an optical device for measuring sugar concentration in a solution) are devices you might consider as you get more serious about your meadmaking. Such tools afford quicker and more accurate measuring capabilities.

Opposite: Primary fermentation occurs in a large food-grade bucket of at least 6 gallons, preferably marked on the outside to indicate volume. Secondary fermentation takes place in a glass carboy with airlock.

Advanced Equipment

As you get more and more into meadmaking, the equipment becomes more advanced on several fronts. Advanced equipment includes tools that make the process easier and tools that afford better measuring capabilities.

- A large funnel that fits into the neck of your fermenters makes it much easier to get liquids like sanitizers into the carboy without making a mess.

- More fermenters allow you to have several different batches in process at the same time; an assortment of sizes is useful as your batch size varies.

- A hand spray bottle can hold sanitizer solution.

- A digital timer keeps track of yeast rehydration duration; alternatively, a timer app for your smartphone can do the same job.

- A wine degasser mounts in an electric hand drill and is used to initially mix the must as well as for periodic stirring (degassing) of the mead. (I use a variable-speed plug-in drill, but some cordless models will also work.)

- A small scale that can measure fractions of a gram is useful for measuring nutrients and other light ingredients; weighing is more accurate than using measuring spoons.

- A large scale capable of measuring up to 25 pounds (12 kilograms) while showing fractions of a pound (fractions of a kilogram) is useful for measuring honey. (Typically a restaurant-style scale works well for this.)

- A bottle corker is handy if you are going to cork bottles; for larger batches, you may want to go with a floor corker, because the hand corkers are tedious and can be problematic when filling several cases at a time.

- A refractometer is an optical device for measuring sugar concentration in a solution; it can measure the sugar level with just a couple of drops of solution in contrast to the ounces you need to fill the hydrometer test jar. There are a couple of considerations related to refractometers for meadmaking. First, many have an upper limit of 28° or 32° Brix/Plato, which is in the 1.120/1.139 specific gravity range, and some meads are bigger than that. If your mead has an original gravity higher than that, you need to do a precise dilution with water before the refractometer will be useful. Second, after fermentation has started, you need to use a calculator to convert the instrument's reading into a true specific gravity value. A quick Google search will help you find a number of online refractometer calculators that can do the calculations for you.

- A wine thief allows you to take a relatively small sample from a carboy.

- A kegging system, either pin-lock or ball-lock, can use CO_2, mixed CO_2 and nitrogen (beer gas), or pure nitrogen; the cylinder for the first is different from that for the other two, and the regulator needs to match the gas cylinder choice. (The regulator used for CO_2 and nitrogen/beer gas is the same except for the connector used to mate the piece to the cylinder. You can typically buy the fitting to convert from one to the other.) The complete setup includes the kegs, the appropriate liquid and gas disconnects, the regulator, the gas cylinder, a tap, and the hoses.

- A plate filter housing and appropriate pads are useful for clarifying. Place a filter between the keg of mead and an empty keg and use gas pressure to force the mead through the filter. A plastic tank and hand pump allow filtration without a kegging system; more expensive filters include a pump to force the mead through the filter.

- A wine acid test kit allows you to measure the total acid level.

- Some pH test strips, available in various ranges, are useful for testing acidity; pH can range from 1 to 14, but most meadmakers look for values in the 3 to 6 range.

- A pH meter (a push-button device to quickly measure the pH of a solution) and the associated calibration and storage solutions are delicate devices that provide an alternative to pH test strips. These devices require proper storage (most with the sensor in a specific storage solution) and periodic recalibration (which is built-in but requires one or sometimes several special calibration solutions).

- If you have a kegging system, a counter pressure bottler allows you to bottle still or carbonated beverages from your kegs. (There are several styles on the market, or you can find plans for making your own.)

- A small medicine dropper is useful when preparing small samples for blending and balance evaluations.

- A graduated cylinder is useful for measuring accurately when blending and making other adjustments.

- A large commercial kitchen-style measuring pitcher—typically 1 gallon (4 liters) or larger—is useful for measuring liquids. Your homebrew supply shop may carry these, or you can try a restaurant supply store.

- An activated charcoal water filter to remove all the chlorine or chloramine from the water will also remove many volatile organic substances that cause odors and flavors, but it will not remove hardness or other dissolved minerals from the water.

THE STEPS

Honey may be difficult to obtain in the exact amount called for here, but if you have a little more or a little less than 14 pounds (6.35 kilograms) of honey, don't worry, the process will still work and will still get you the target original gravity. You will just be making a little more or a little less than the target 5 gallons (19 liters) of mead. To help you estimate the change in volume, we are using about 2.8 pounds of honey per gallon (1 kilogram of honey per 2.98 liters) of mead. If for example, if you had 12 pounds (5.44 kilograms) of honey, the volume of your batch would be reduced to just over 4.29 gallons (16.3 liters).

PREPARING THE MUST

1. Pour the honey into the large fermenter, using the sanitized spatula to scrape the residual honey from the container. Tare the scale to account for the fermenter and add the amount of honey the recipe calls for. If necessary, use the measuring cup to rinse the honey container with a little of the water from the bucket treated with the Campden tablet. Return the measuring cup to the sanitizer bucket. If the honey container has a resealable cover, put it back on and then shake to dissolve the honey. If the honey container isn't resealable, just stir the water with the sanitized spoon to dissolve the residual honey before pouring it into the fermenter with the honey. Before adding this honey-water mixture, be sure to take note of where the pure honey reaches on the calibrated fermenter. We'll want to account for the water added at this stage so that we don't add too much water in the next step.

2. Add approximately 2 gallons (8 liters) of the water treated with the Campden tablet into the bucket with the honey. (The exact amount is not important.) Using the sanitized large spoon, stir the honey and water until it is well mixed and there are no clumps of thick honey at the bottom of the fermenter. Leave the spoon in the bucket with the honey and water.

3. Using your sanitized hydrometer test jar, or by simply dropping the hydrometer into the fermenter, take a hydrometer reading. Specific gravity should be much higher than 1.115 and may even be off the scale, depending on your hydrometer. Add several more cups of water to the mixture and stir to blend. Again, note the hydrometer reading. Keep adding a little water, stirring, and then reading the hydrometer. As you get closer to 1.115 on the hydrometer, add smaller quantities of water. Stop when the hydrometer reads 1.115.

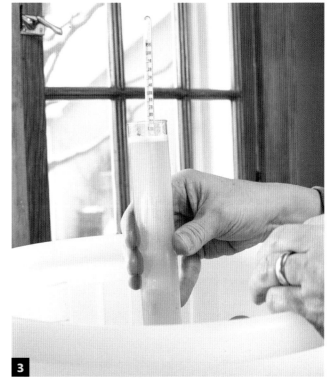

4. Place the thermometer in the honey and water mixture. When the reading stabilizes, record the temperature in your log. Remove the thermometer, rinse it in the Campden tablet–treated water, and then return it to the sanitizer solution before placing the sanitized cover on the fermenter.

PREPARING THE YEAST

1. Place about 4 ounces (120 milliliters) of the Campden tablet–treated water in the measuring cup and put the cup in the microwave for a few seconds—the water needs to be hot but doesn't need to boil. Then, with the sanitized thermometer placed in the glass, slowly add a small amount of the room-temperature, Campden tablet–treated water to get the temperature of the water in the measuring cup to 104°F (40°C). A couple of degrees cooler is OK, but don't go over 104°F (40°C).

2. Add the Go-Ferm to the warm water in the glass and using the small spoon, stir to dissolve it. The Go-Ferm tends to clump in the water; I find it easiest to press the lumps to the side of the glass and stir a lot.

3. Add the packet of yeast to the water and Go-Ferm and stir to suspend the yeast. Cover with a piece of plastic cling wrap and note the time; you want the yeast to be rehydrating in the glass with the Go-Ferm for at least 15 minutes but no more than 20 minutes.

4. While waiting for the yeast to rehydrate, put the 4 grams (approximately $1/2$ teaspoon plus $1/3$ teaspoon, 0.14 ounce by weight) of Fermaid K and 8 grams (approximately $1^2/_3$ teaspoons, 0.28 ounce by weight) of diammonium phosphate into the plastic bag and shake to mix the two. Record the quantities in your log. Add 2 grams (approximately ¾ teaspoon, 0.071 ounce by weight) of the mixture to the fermenter containing the honey and water and record it in your log.

5. Stir the yeast mixture to resuspend the yeast and then pour the entire contents of the glass into the bucket with the honey mixture. Stir and place the cover on the bucket. Record in your log the date and time the yeast was pitched.

PRIMARY FERMENTATION

Keep the bucket with the honey mixture at room temperature, or about 62–75°F (17–24°C). You will need to stir the fermenting honey 2–3 times a day for the next 8 days. In a perfect world, that means roughly every 8–12 hours. Do your best every day even if you can't keep a regular schedule for the stirrings. Stir gently initially; the motion will cause a lot of foam, but it tends to take a few seconds to build up. Each time you stir, stir until no new foam forms, and then record the date and time in your log. Place a sanitized hydrometer into the fermenter before you start stirring to get a current reading for the log. On days 3, 5, and 7 (2, 4, and 6 days, respectively, after the initial batch was started) add to the fermenter another 2 grams (approximately ¾ teaspoon, 0.071 ounce by weight) of the Fermaid K and diammonium phosphate mixture from the plastic bag. Don't add the mixture until after you have completed one of the day's stirring sessions. Record the addition in your log. Also, continue the stirring process but do not stir after day 8.

SECONDARY FERMENTATION

1. On day 21, lift the bucket of mead onto a table, tall chair, or countertop. (You need enough height to be able to siphon the mead into the carboy.) Add a few cups (1 liter) of the sanitizer solution to the carboy and slosh it around, making sure the entire inside of the carboy is sanitized. Drain the residual solution in the carboy into the bucket of sanitizer and place the carboy on the floor below the bucket of mead.

2. Sanitize the carboy stopper, airlock, autosiphon, and racking hose next. Make sure the autosiphon and racking hose are completely wet by the solution before draining them—insert the auto siphon into the bucket of mead and attach the racking hose to one end.

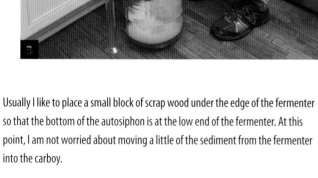

Usually I like to place a small block of scrap wood under the edge of the fermenter so that the bottom of the autosiphon is at the low end of the fermenter. At this point, I am not worried about moving a little of the sediment from the fermenter into the carboy.

3. Place the hydrometer sample jar on the floor next to the carboy. Use the autosiphon's pump to start the transfer, then gently let the mead run out of the hose into the hydrometer sample jar. Once the jar is nearly full, place your sanitized finger over the end of the hose and carefully insert the hose into the carboy. (You want the tip of the hose to reach to the bottom.) Let the mead transfer, and when the siphon stops, remove the hose from the carboy and insert the stopper with the airlock. Record the date and time in your log as a racking of the mead to a carboy. Place the hydrometer jar in the sink and then gently lower the hydrometer into the jar. Record the reading in your log. Place the thermometer in the hydrometer jar and record the temperature of the mead in your log.

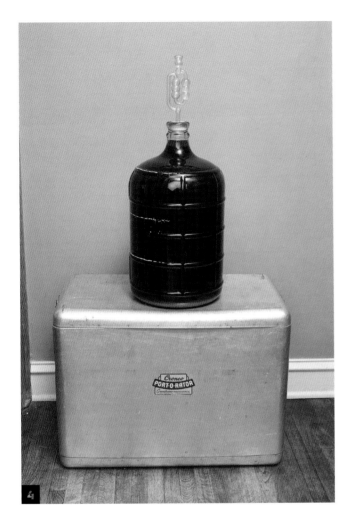

4. Move the carboy of mead to a room-temperature space out of direct light and look at it every few days. The bubbles through the airlock should slow way down until you see less than one per minute. The mead may also start to clarify as the yeast drops out of suspension.

5. Once the mead has started to clarify and the specific gravity (checked with the hydrometer) hasn't changed over several days, sanitize the stopper and neck of the carboy by pouring a small amount of the sanitizer solution over them with a small spoon. Prepare the Super-Kleer K.C. Finings (packaged as two separate liquids in a larger pouch: packet D1 is the smaller, and packet D2 is the larger) by dipping the whole package in the sanitizer solution. Sanitize the scissors and measuring cup, as well, by dipping them into the sanitizer solution. (Leave a few ounces of solution in the measuring cup.) Remove the stopper and airlock from the carboy and place them in the sanitizer solution in the measuring cup. Clip the corner of packet D1 off with the sanitized scissors and squeeze the liquid from the packet into the carboy before replacing the stopper and airlock. Gently swirl the carboy to mix. Note the date and time in your log.

Roughly 1 hour later, start preparing packet D2 by placing it in the sanitizer solution. Sanitize the small glass, the small spoon, the scissors, the stopper and neck of the carboy (using the small spoon), and the inside of the measuring cup in the bucket of sanitizer solution, making sure all are thoroughly clean. Leave a few ounces (100 milliliters) of solution in the measuring cup. Remove the stopper and airlock from the carboy and place them in the sanitizer solution in the measuring cup. Remove the glass from the sanitizer and put approximately 1 ounce (30 milliliters) of warm tap water in the glass. Clip the corner of packet D2 with the scissors and squeeze the contents into the glass of water. Use the sanitized spoon to mix. Pour the contents of the glass into the carboy and replace the stopper and airlock. Gently swirl the carboy to get the packet D2 solution mixed into the mead. Note the date and time in your log, and within a day or two the mead should become clear.

BOTTLING

If you have a kegging system, you can skip bottling; just siphon the mead into a sanitized keg and you are ready to go. However, if you are bottling, follow these steps:

1. Gently place the carboy of clear mead on the counter or table. You need enough height to be able to siphon the mead into the bottles.

2. Sanitize the bottles by pouring a few ounces (100 milliliters) of sanitizer solution into a bottle and, while holding your sanitized thumb over the top, shaking the bottle to wet the entire inside. Dump the sanitizer back into the bucket and set the bottle on the floor with the mouth up. Repeat for the remaining bottles. Sanitize the bottle caps, the hydrometer sample jar, the measuring cup, and the bottling wand in the bucket of sanitizer solution. Be sure the entire inside and outside of the wand is wet by the sanitizer. Drain the sanitizer solution from the hydrometer jar and the measuring cup and place them on the floor. Sanitize the autosiphon and racking hose; make sure both are completely wet. Drain the autosiphon, racking hose, and bottling wand. Insert the siphon into the bucket of mead. Attach one end of the racking hose to the autosiphon and the other to the bottling wand.

3. Use the autosiphon's pump to start the transfer of the mead, gently letting it run out of the bottling wand into the hydrometer sample jar. Once the sample jar is nearly full, you can place the bottling wand in the sanitized measuring cup while you get ready to fill the bottles. Insert the bottling wand into a sanitized bottle and remove it when the mead reaches the top of the bottle. Place a sanitized cap on the top of the bottle and continue filling more bottles until all the mead is bottled. You may end up with a partial bottle at the end—no sense bothering to cap that one because it will oxidize quickly; you'll have to drink it when you finish bottling.

The bottling wand typically has a small peg on the bottom. When pressed against the bottom of the bottle, this peg allows the mead to flow into the bottle. When you lift the wand from the bottom of the bottle, the peg should stop the flow of mead.

4. I prefer to crimp (seal) the caps while I have the bottles on the table or counter. Gently lift the bottles onto the table or counter and crimp the cap using the bottle capper. Repeat for the remaining bottles and then record the bottling date and the number of bottles in your log.

Place the hydrometer sample jar in the sink and gently lower the hydrometer into it; record the reading in your log. Place the thermometer in the sample jar. Once the temperature reading stabilizes, record the temperature in your log.

5. You can mark the caps with a permanent marker with a code for the batch. (Be sure to note the code in your log.) Alternatively, you can print small labels on ¾-inch round stickers with your computer and printer, then stick those on the caps. A final option is to place some sort of label on the side of the bottle—I just print small rectangular labels on the computer, cut them to size, and glue them on with a child-safe glue stick.

CHAPTER

6

FINISHING YOUR MEAD

HAZE DEVELOPS FROM SOLIDS SUSPENDED IN A MEAD. Most of the yeast cells will eventually fall to the bottom, given enough time. Highly flocculent yeast strains drop faster than nonflocculent strains. Haze can also be induced by the honey itself or the fruit or spices you added to the mead.

Most people enjoy clear meads more than cloudy meads. There are a few different finishing approaches to getting a clear mead.

THE WAITING GAME

Just waiting for the mead to clarify on its own is the cheapest and easiest finishing method, but it can be hard to predict how long it will take for the mead to clear. Further, since your carboy will be unavailable until the mead clears, you have an indirect cost: waiting keeps you from using the carboy for your next batch of mead.

If you are going to leave your mead in a carboy for an extended time to clarify, you need to make sure the carboy has virtually no headspace to minimize oxidation (see page 60 for instructions). I usually don't like to water down my meads for storage, but another alternative to minimize the headspace is to top off the carboy with boiled and chilled water. Finally, while the carboy is sitting, you need to periodically check and top off the airlock. Bulk aging in a keg is one way to avoid oxidation concerns; just keep a little gas pressure on the keg to keep the lid sealed.

Winemakers tend to use sulfur dioxide in their wines while bulk aging for extended periods of time as a means of minimizing oxidation. You need to use a sulfur dioxide test kit, sold at most homebrew supply stores, to be sure you have the proper level, but since I don't bulk age in carboys, I have not tried this.

FINING AGENTS

You can purchase many different fining agents at your homebrew supply store. In addition to clarifying mead, you can use them to reduce astringency, reduce bitterness, remove off odors, and even remove browning caused by oxidation. However, there can be some side effects, including removing color, reducing body, reducing flavor, and reducing aroma.

Most of the suspended particles in the mead have an electrical charge, either positive or negative, and many fining agents also have an electrical charge. Electrically charged fining agents will be attracted to particles of the opposite charge, and as they collect together, they will become heavier and eventually will sink to the bottom. Fining agents with no electrical charge work by absorption—sort of like a sponge that soaks up haze-causing particles—and then sink to the bottom.

In the commercial beer-brewing industry, where most of the research on fining agents has been performed, brewers add the fining agents at the lowest temperature the beer will see after production, perhaps in part because a clear beer may develop a haze (chill haze) after being chilled below the fining temperature. For mead, the rule still makes sense, even though most meads are not going to suffer from a chill haze as beers do.

Commercially available fining agents in your local homebrew supply store include gelatin, isinglass, bentonite, Sparkolloid, carbon (activated charcoal), pectic enzyme, kieselsol, and chitosan. I use Super-Kleer K.C. Finings to clarify mead.

SUPER-KLEER K.C. FININGS

These come packaged in two pouches: D1, which contains kieselsol and an inert silica gel (with a negative charge), and D2, which contains chitosan, a nonallergenic polymer derived from shells of crustaceans (with a positive charge). Chapter 5 gives instructions on how to use Super-Kleer. It normally works within a day or two and sometimes starts to show results within a few hours. All the kieselsol and chitosan are left in the sediment at the bottom of the carboy with the yeast cells. When mixing the two packets, I gently rock the carboy to get a swirling action started; violent stirring is not wanted or needed. Although many meadmakers add finings as the temperature rises, I generally add Super-Kleer at fermentation temperature and find that the meads stay clear even when chilled later.

GELATIN

This is a positively charged protein usually derived from animal products. It can be used to reduce tannins (a cause of astringency) in a mead. Negatively charged tannins are attracted to the gelatin and then sink to the bottom. Unfortunately, excess gelatin can cause a haze, but you can avoid that by using kieselsol a day or two after you add the gelatin. The negatively charged kieselsol works to reduce the excess gelatin and create a clearer mead with reduced astringency. Preparation requires soaking a typical dose of gelatin (1 teaspoon per 5 gallons) in 4 ounces of cool water for 1 hour, then stirring it vigorously and bringing it to a boil before mixing it into the mead. Gelatin works slowly; wait about two weeks before racking off the sediment.

ISINGLASS

Extracted from the swim bladders of fish, isinglass is a positively charged protein traditionally used as a clarifier in English cask-conditioned beers. I don't recommend using isinglass to clarify a mead with a heavy haze, but it can be useful to get final brilliant clarity if other agents have failed. Isinglass—a gentle agent that does not strip flavor or aroma from the mead—is an alternative to filtering, which generally strips more character from the mead. Multiple vendors sell it in many forms, including liquids, powder, paste, and dried flakes, so you need to follow the vendor's directions for dosage. Liquid forms of isinglass deteriorate rapidly at temperatures over 68°F (20°C), and different sources of isinglass exhibit different behavior at the same pH. (Generally, if the pH is below 3.4, action is significantly reduced.) Also, if the mead has little or no tannin, you must add tannin for the isinglass to be effective. (¼ to ½ teaspoon of powdered tannin per 5 gallons of mead can be added before or after the isinglass.)

BENTONITE

This negatively charged fining agent is made from a type of clay first found at Fort Benton, Wyoming. It is frequently used by winemakers in the initial fermentation to help strip out positively charged particles in the must. Fermentation bubbles keep the bentonite particles stirred, and each time they sink to the bottom, they take a few more positively charged particles with them. It is not as effective during the post-fermentation cycle, because it will quickly sink to the bottom of the fermenter unless you stir it several times a day. Meads may contain heat-unstable proteins that coagulate when exposed to excessive fluctuating temperatures, and that may create a haze in a bottle of clear mead after it has been exposed to temperature variations. In winemaking, bentonite is commonly used to prevent these hazes, but I have not found it necessary to use bentonite in my meads, perhaps because I don't bottle many meads and I avoid temperature fluctuations of the finished mead. When using bentonite post-fermentation, you need to keep the mead at room temperature for 10–14 days before racking off the sediment; if you chill while waiting for the mead to clarify, some of the bentonite will go into suspension and reduce the flavor complexity of the finished mead, as well as remove some of the color from the mead.

SPARKOLLOID

Made from a blend of diatomaceous earth and polysaccharides, Sparkolloid is a proprietary fining agent effective in removing fine suspended particles. Sparkolloid has a reputation for not stripping character from mead if used at the proper dosage. The powder must first be prepared by boiling the recommended dose with some water; the hot solution is then added to the mead while stirring. It can take a long time for all the Sparkolloid to settle out after the addition—some people claim it takes 3–6 months to drop out of suspension—so I have not used Sparkolloid in a long time.

CARBON

Activated charcoal has no electrical charge and is not used much as a fining agent but more as an agent to remove odors, flavors, and colors. It can absorb the brown color and odors caused by oxidation, but you need to be careful, because it will also remove the desirable colors, flavors, and aromas. Perhaps because of the potential negative side effects, carbon does not appear to be as widely available as most other fining agents. I would use carbon only as a last resort.

PECTINASE

Technically, this enzyme is not a fining agent. It clarifies a mead suffering from pectic haze by breaking down the pectin, a naturally occurring substance in most plants that allows you to make jelly from fruit. Pectic enzyme is best added during primary fermentation to prevent pectic haze in fruit meads. Its action tends to be slower in the presence of ethanol. Follow the package recommendations for the amount to add; too much is better than too little. When adding at the end of fermentation, you want to keep the mead around 70°F (21°C) and wait about four days for the enzyme to work.

KIESELSOL

This negatively charged agent, also known as silicon dioxide, increases the negative charge of other suspended particles, making positively charged fining agents more effective. Kieselsol can also remove some bitter phenolic flavors in mead. You typically use kieselsol

You can test to see if a haze is caused by pectins by mixing 1 teaspoon of the mead with 4 teaspoons of denatured (rubbing) alcohol in a small container. Shake to mix and let it sit for a few hours. If a solid forms in the container, then the mead contains pectins and would benefit from the addition of pectic enzymes.

with chitosan (as in Super-Kleer) or with gelatin, but when you use it with gelatin, add the gelatin a day or two before the kieselsol is added.

CHITOSAN

This positively charged agent is composed of chitin, a structural component of the shells of crustaceans. When used with kieselsol (as in Super-Kleer), it can very effectively remove most suspended particles. It is a gentle agent that has minimal impact on the flavor and aroma of the mead.

CHILLING

Chilling a mead to 32–40°F (0–4°C) will accelerate the dropping of the suspended particles, including yeast cells. If you cold-condition your mead in a carboy, you can easily determine when the mead clarifies. Once it is clear, you can transfer it to another carboy or gently handle the carboy with the sediment when you get ready to package the mead.

If you cold-condition in a keg, you have to use a keg tap to extract a little mead when you want to check for clarity; you also need to be aware that the liquid-out tube in the standard keg goes nearly to the bottom and may be dispensing most of the sediment from the bottom in the first few ounces poured. Some meadmakers remove the bottom inch or so of the liquid-out tube from the keg they use for cold-conditioning their meads to avoid that concern. Once the mead is clear, you need to carefully transfer it to a sanitized serving keg, leaving the sediment behind in the original keg.

During aging, tartaric acid tends to form harmless, tasteless, odorless tartrate crystals that can look like broken glass. (These are sometimes called "wine diamonds" in the wine world.) Cold-conditioning, generally for a few weeks at around 32–40°F (0–4°C), can reduce or eliminate the later formation of tartrate crystals (potassium bitartrate) in some pyments and overly acidic meads as the mead ages. The process is called "chill proofing" in the winemaking world.

FILTERING

Several filtering devices originally developed for home winemakers can be used to make mead. While the more complex filtering systems include an electrically powered pump as part of the mechanism, simpler filters contain just a filter media in a housing of some sort, and then you have to transfer the mead through the filter media using either a hand pump or gas pressure in a kegging system. The filter media in a typical home winemaking filter is not reusable; once the media has been wet by the mead, it cannot be safely removed from the housing and saved for filtering a future batch. However, if you have several batches of mead to filter at the same time, you can keep using the media until finished or until the filter gets too plugged to allow the mead to pass through.

Most home filtering systems are available with at least three different grades of media, typically called coarse, medium, and sterile, with each successive grade removing finer (smaller) particles. Start by filtering the mead with the coarse media, then the medium, and finally the sterile; skipping the progression may result in the filter getting plugged before you get the entire batch filtered. The sterile grade is tight enough to remove yeast and bacteria. You can always stop after any of these grades, though, because while each successive degree removes more particulate matter from the mead, it also removes more flavor and aroma characteristics. (I have rarely used the sterile media.)

I use the gas pressure in my kegging system to force the mead out of the liquid-out connection on one keg through the filter and into another sanitized keg. In operation, I sanitize the filter housing and associated hoses with Star San solution and then immerse the filter pads in Star San as well. After assembling the now sanitized components, I have to purge the sanitizer from the filter with my mead, so I end up discarding the first mead that runs out of the filter until I am sure the flow includes just mead. If you are filtering several different meads in succession, you will need to discard the first runnings each time you switch the mead flowing to the filter, because the first few ounces will be a mixture of previous mead and the current mead.

Start with the kegging system set on the lowest gas pressure that will still get the mead through the filter and increase pressure as the filter media starts to get plugged. As you increase the pressure, you may also find leaks in the filter housing that require you to tighten connections to avoid spraying mead everywhere. You can stop the input to the filter at any time by removing the liquid disconnect from the liquid-out side of the input keg. When monitoring the first runnings to be sure I've flushed the sanitizer, I find it easiest to remove the threaded disconnect from the output hose of the filter and let the liquid flow into a large glass or pitcher. When the runnings are just the mead, I disconnect from the input keg, reattach the disconnect to the output hose, attach the disconnect to the new keg, and then reconnect the input side to the input keg. It may sound complicated, but it isn't.

BALANCE

Balance in a mead is not a simple two-sided thing like a playground seesaw. On a seesaw, each person can influence the balance with his or her weight and distance from the center. Balance in a mead, however, has many dimensions and may differ based on the taster.

The components used to balance a mead address aroma, flavor, structure, sweetness, and the mouthfeel aspects of body and carbonation. Balance requires a synergy of all these aspects of the mead. All the characteristics do not have to be at the same intensity level, but none should overshadow one another to the point that the mead becomes one-dimensional.

The simplest aspect of balance involves sweetness and acidity, but a single correct amount of sweetness that will yield the proper sugar-acid balance in a mead can't be determined using an equation, and other aspects of balance will also play against the sweetness and the acidity. A mead with too little sweetness for the acid will seem harsh, sharp, and acidic. A mead with too much sweetness for the acid will seem sugary, cloying, and flabby. Meads with too much sweetness and too much acid are frequently said to have a "sweet-tart" character after the classic candy SweetTarts. Sweet-tart meads are frequently the result of trying to balance a highly acidic mead by back-sweetening with honey; these meads don't work because other aspects of the meads (usually the honey) don't work with the sweetness and acid levels.

You also should consider the balance among acidity, sweetness, and tannin, as well as the balance between the sweetness and the honey character. Alcohol has a balance between acidity and tannin, and there is also a balance between the honey character and the other special ingredients such as fruit and spices. Balance must consider mouthfeel aspects like carbonation and body.

The components of balance have different intensities in different styles of mead. A sweet mead has to be sweeter than a dry mead, but both must be balanced, so the sweet mead will need more acidity, tannin, and/or alcohol to achieve balance. Different styles of mead will have different alcohol levels, different carbonation levels, and different sweetness levels. While a wide range is possible, the resulting mead needs to have an enjoyable balance.

COMPONENTS OF BALANCE
Balance addresses sweetness, acidity, tannins, alcohols, honeys, carbonation, and body.

SWEETNESS
Sweetness comes from the residual sugar in a mead, generally from the honey but possibly from other ingredients (fruits, other adjuncts, or even techniques such as wood aging). Sweetness is mainly a flavor characteristic, but we can sense sweetness in aroma as well. Residual sweetness mainly comes from the sugars that survived through fermentation, which can be controlled by manually stopping the fermentation short of complete attenuation or by adding honey or sweet adjuncts after fermentation has finished. (Uncontrolled additions of fermentables to a "finished" fermentation may restart the fermentation.)

The BJCP taxonomy includes dry, semisweet, and sweet meads, but the lines between them are not absolute. A dry mead does not have to be bone-dry, and a sweet mead does not have to be syrupy-sweet like a dessert wine. The borders of semisweet are ambiguous on both the dry side and on the sweet side.

In sweet meads, the sweetness needs to assume a dominant role in the characteristics of the mead, but the mead still should not be cloying. A semisweet mead should have noticeable sweetness, but the sweetness should not dominate. Dry meads will have little to no noticeable sweetness. In dry mead it is easy to confuse fruity esters with sweetness, since many esters are slightly sweet.

As residual sugar content increases, the body of the mead will also increase. However, even a dry mead has to have some body. The sweetness of a mead needs to be independent of the strength (original gravity) of the mead.

ACIDITY

Acidity refers to the perception of acid in the mead. As a component of the mead's structure, it can be related to the pH and can be described as tart or sour at some levels. Acid should not be a primary flavor in a mead, but should play a supporting role by adding complexity to the overall structure.

Honey has gluconic acid as a natural ingredient, but acid levels in honey vary between honey varieties, seasons, and even regions. Fermentation will naturally add acid to the mead, lowering the pH, and different yeast strains have different impacts on the pH during fermentation. More acid will be introduced by fruit additions as well.

Acidity can be increased post-fermentation by adding citric acid, malic acid, tartaric acid, or "acid blend" comprising a mixture of the three acids. You can remove excess acid chemically, but this can be somewhat problematic, because the byproducts of the process can be undesirable. Chill proofing (storage below 40°F or 4°C) will work to precipitate excess tartaric acid in some meads.

TANNINS

Tannins are bitter-tasting polyphenols that also bind to and precipitate proteins in the mead. Tannins have an astringent mouthfeel and can become mouth-puckering at sufficient levels. (One common description of astringent mouthfeel is that it is like sucking on grape skins.) The large tannin molecules can also create a drying aftertaste. Because they are not volatile, they do not have an aroma, but the source of the tannins may well have an associated aroma.

Honey does not naturally have tannins, but you can add tannins with fruits, spices, teas, chemical adjuncts (typically tannin extracts), or wood aging. Many berries have significant tannin content, the highest concentration typically coming from the skins and seeds of the fruit (one reason many mead recipes calling for fruit advise not to crush the seeds).

Beers are called dry when they have little residual sugar, but for meads and wines, dry can mean a lack of residual sugar or can indicate the drink has sufficient tannin to offset the sugars. Tannins contribute to balance by making a mead seem dry even if there is residual sugar present. Thus dryness cannot be determined just by using a hydrometer.

Adding tannin to a mead can be fairly simple, but removing it is not. (See the discussion of finings earlier in this chapter for approaches to removing tannins.) Balancing excess tannin can be difficult, because adding too much sweetness (the main counterbalancing aspect) may upset other parts of the balance.

ALCOHOLS

Alcohols are fermentation byproducts, and ethanol should be the dominant alcohol in mead. Ethanol has a strongly sharp aroma, as well as a sharp flavor that can be bitter and sweet to some people. Since ethanol is also a versatile solvent, it will often carry other volatile characteristics. Alcohols will impart a warming mouthfeel to beverages, and the warmth generally increases as the level is increased.

In the BJCP taxonomy, the alcohol level increases from hydromel to standard to sack. Standard-strength meads are defined as similar to table wine at 7–14 percent ABV (according to U.S. law).

Somewhat like sweetness, alcohol content is managed by controlling the amount of fermentable sugar and the amount of attenuation during the fermentation. The fermentables may come from fruits, sugars, and even malt as well as from honey. While the *potential* may be increased, achieving the attenuation needed to realize that potential may require a more attentuative yeast strain and may even require diligently managing the fermentation. Generally, more fermentables in the mead will produce more alcohols, but stopping fermentation before the yeast has finished will result in a lower alcohol level than indicated by the potential and will also leave more residual (unfermented) sugars that will add sweetness to the mead.

Meads are rarely adjusted to modify the alcohol levels. The alcohol level can be lowered by dilution, but that also impacts most other aspects of the meads. The alcohol level can be raised by adding neutral distilled spirits, but this is typically done only for fortified meads.

HONEYS

Honeys vary in the flavor and aroma they impart, and intense honey flavors are generally desirable in meads. Some varietal honeys have strong characteristics from the nectar source. Strongly sweet honeys, such as tupelo honey, tend to seem sweet even when fermented dry, and the strong honey flavors or aromas of some honey varietals are more noticeable and often make you think of sweetness even when it may not be present.

The honey aspect of balance can be controlled through the choice of honey varietal and the amount of honey used in the mead. More honey results in more character, but the strong honey character can be reduced by using a mix of varietals, including one with a lower character. A mead with more residual sugar will have a stronger honey character than one fermented drier, because more unfermented honey will remain. Strong, sweeter meads will naturally have more honey character than weaker, drier meads, but back-sweetening a finished mead with more honey will increase the honey character.

CARBONATION

Carbonation is just dissolved carbon dioxide that adds acidity (as carbonic acid) to the mead. Carbonation is a part of mouthfeel, but it can also make the body of the mead seem lighter. In the BJCP taxonomy, meads are still, petillant, or sparkling, but again, there isn't a firm border between the three. A still mead may have a few bubbles. Sparkling meads don't gush, but they may range from mouth-filling like many beers to sodalike or even champagnelike. Petillant meads fill the gap between the two extremes with light carbonation.

BODY

Body refers to the viscosity of the mead or the thickness in the mouthfeel. In the BJCP taxonomy, typical terms for body are *light*, *medium*, and *full*, but defective meads may be described with terms outside that range. For example, descriptors like *thin* or *watery* can be applied to meads with very light body. Extremely full-bodied meads may be described with terms like *syrupy*, *viscous*, or *thick*.

Selecting a different honey varietal can cause slight changes in the body of a mead. Higher attenuation will generally reduce the body, while lowering attenuation will increase the body. Final gravity adjustments can be used to modify the body but will impact the sweetness and alcohols in the balance. Back-sweetening after fermentation can increase the body, and higher tannin content tends to also increase the perception of body.

PUTTING IT ALL TOGETHER

When you hear meadmakers and winemakers talking about structure or backbone, they usually mean a combination of acidity and tannins. The sweetness-acidity-tannin balance has the most impact on the drinkability of a mead. You can improve the balance of an overly sweet mead by increasing either the acidity or the tannins or even by increasing both, but remember that the structure (tannins and acidity) also needs to work with the alcohol level to result in a pleasant mead.

A mead with too much acidity can be improved by increasing the sweetness—or by reducing the acidity, which is generally more difficult. When increasing the sweetness, you can add raw honey, but I prefer to blend in a much sweeter mead—much sweeter so as to not overly dilute the other aspects of the mead—because it yields a softer character to the mead. To reduce the acidity, products available to home winemakers will work in mead as well. (Follow the package directions.) In meads where the acidity comes from malic and/or citric acids, you can use a malolactic fermentation (MLF) by lactic acid bacteria to convert the malic acid into softer lactic acid and the citric acid into diacetyl, a compound often described as buttery. To me, the results of a MLF are too unpredictable, so I would just blend in a nonacidic mead if back-sweetening isn't enough to balance.

Acidity, tannin, and alcohol together balance the perception of sweetness and honey, but the combination of acidity and tannin (the structure) has to roughly balance the alcohol. If there is not enough structure for the alcohol, the mead will be flabby, soft, and heavy. If there is too much structure for the alcohol, the mead will be astringent and tart.

Tannins and acidity are somewhat interchangeable in that both can be used to balance sweetness and honey character. If less acidity is used for balance more tannin can be used. If more acidity is used for balance, less tannin can be used. If both tannins and acidity are too high, the mead will be harshly astringent. A number of varieties of tannin are now available to home winemakers to increase structure, many formulated for post-fermentation use. Follow the instructions, including any guidance on how long you should wait to package after adding the tannin to allow any excess to settle out. Gelatin, discussed under fining agents, is a good choice for removing tannins.

A mead with low honey character and low acidity will be boring, while a mead with higher honey intensity and proper sweetness and structure will be comparatively luscious. A mead with high acidity and low sweetness will seem tart, while a mead with high sweetness compared to acidity will seem soft and flabby. What it all means is that generally there are several ways to balance a mead, but you may not be able to fully balance a mead using just one technique, and a technique that works for one mead may not work for another mead if the ingredients are not identical.

7 PACKAGING

YOU HAVE FINISHED FERMENTING YOUR MEAD and have made any post-fermentation adjustments. Now you need to package it and empty your fermenter so you can start another batch of mead.

Two main packaging approaches are readily available to home meadmakers, the first using glass bottles similar to those used for beer or wine, and the second using the corny keg employed by many home beer-makers. The corny keg requires more initial investment in equipment, but the equipment is easy to use and reusable.

BOTTLING

Beer and wine generally are packaged in bottles, and this is a viable option for packaging mead. Beer bottles use a crown cap that needs to be crimped onto the bottle with a bottle capper. For wine bottles, a cork is typically inserted with one of several types of corking devices, ranging from relatively cheap but difficult to use to more expensive and easier to use. Some sparkling wines come in bottles that also support a crown cap in addition to a cork.

For still meads, the classic wine bottle sealed with a cork will work nicely, as will bottles sealed with a crown cap. I don't recommend using a simple cork in a wine bottle for sparkling meads. You need a cork enclosed in a wire cage (similar to corks used for champagne) that helps it stay in the bottle. Basic home corkers cannot insert the type of corks needed for sparkling meads, so you need a more advanced corker. You also need a bottle that can handle the carbonation pressure. Typically, wine bottles that can take the pressure of carbonation have a punted bottom. (The bottom bulges up in the center.) The standard beer bottle can also tolerate the pressure of carbonation—at least the pressure at typical beer carbonation levels.

Generally, plastic bottles are not recommended for long-term storage of mead, because plastic can allow the slow infiltration of oxygen, which will cause the mead to deteriorate. Some of the newer plastic bottles being sold for homemade beer claim to have an oxygen barrier incorporated into the plastic, but I have not tried using them for mead.

Bottling a sparkling mead requires an extra step. The carboy usually has a little sediment (spent yeast and other particles from the honey) on the bottom that you don't want to transfer to the bottles. First, put some priming sugar and a couple of cups (0.5 liter) of water into a small saucepan on the stove and boil it for about 5 minutes. Pour the hot mixture into the bottom of a sanitized bucket and then siphon the mead on top, leaving the sediment behind. Swirl the bucket to be sure the sugar solution gets evenly mixed into the mead and then bottle from the bucket.

The basic method for bottling mead involves using a siphon hose with the bottling wand inserted into the end. Alternatively, you can use a bucket with a drain spigot installed; you attach the hose to the bottling wand and to the drain and then turn the valve on to start the flow of mead. The bottling wand includes a small peg on the bottom that controls a built-in valve. Pressing the wand against the bottom of the bottle opens the valve and allows mead to flow into the bottle. When you lift up on the wand (so it no longer touches the bottom of the bottle) the flow stops.

When using beer bottles, my preference is to sanitize enough bottles and caps for the batch all at once. Then as I fill a single bottle I just lay the bottle cap on the top of the bottle. Once I have filled all the bottles, I then crimp the caps one at a time.

You can sanitize bottles with Star San solution by partially filling a bottle and swirling the solution around to wet the entire inside before draining the bottle back into the sanitizer bucket. Leave the bottles standing upright next to where you are going to do the bottling. A bottle rinser, a device the squirts sanitizer into an inverted bottle, makes this quick work. An alternative technique for sanitizing bottles, if you have an automatic dishwasher with a sanitize cycle, is to place all the bottles (neck down) in the dishwasher. Run the machine on the "sanitize" cycle using no detergent, and when the cycle completes, the bottles will be hot and sanitized.

When using wine bottles, I prefer, again, to sanitize all the bottles and corks (or crowns) at once. However, I cork each bottle as I go. If I'm crowning bottles, either over the cork or with just crowns, I can place the cap on the bottle and then wait until all the bottles are full before crimping each cap down.

UTILITY OR PRESENTATION?

When you decide how to bottle your mead, ultimately you need to decide if you want just a utilitarian package or if you are packaging for show. Utilitarian packages like 12-ounce (330–375 milliliter) brown beer bottles are great for storing your mead and will be expected if you want to enter most homemade mead competitions. The crown caps will very slowly allow some oxygen to infiltrate the seal, however, so if you plan to keep your bottles for a long time, you should consider using the oxygen-barrier type of caps with a special treatment incorporated into the plastic liner that helps reduce oxygen deterioration. An additional option for crowned bottles that you want to keep for a long time is to insert a cork into the bottle and then a crown over the top of the bottle. Using both the cork and the crown gives you a better barrier against oxygen penetration.

Utilitarian packages like ubiquitous 12-ounce (330–375 milliliter) brown beer bottles are great for storing mead (and will, in fact, be expected if you want to enter most homemade mead competitions).

Above: Brown bottles also have the advantage of taking readily available crown-style caps used with a lever-style capper. Consider using the oxygen-barrier variety. An autosiphon like that shown here is another must-have tool for meadmaking.

Right: For presentation-style packaging, you can consider unusual bottle shapes and styles, unusual colors of glass, and fancy seals.

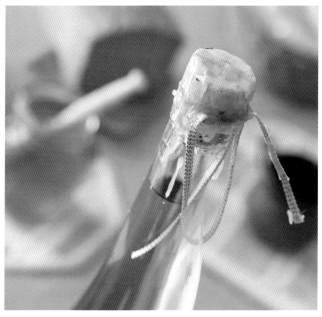

For presentation-style packaging, you can consider unusual bottle shapes and styles, unusual colors of glass, and fancy seals. For example, there are swing-top bottles that have a strong wire mechanism that locks down a plastic or ceramic cap. These bottles are available in various sizes and in several colors of glass and can be resealed by hand.

Once your mead is bottled, you still have presentation options. Most homemade beer/wine/mead shops offer colorful plastic hoods that resemble those on commercial wine bottles. Typically, the hoods are applied and then shrunk into place with steam or hot air. Most shops also sell colorful wax or paraffin seals; you heat according to the instructions and then dip the neck of each bottle into the molten material to form a fancy seal. I used a colorful wax-type seal on swing-top bottles for some mead I donated to a charity auction.

Your final consideration involves labeling the bottles. As a utilitarian approach, you can put the whole batch in a box or two and just mark the box. For a little nicer option, you can print a few descriptive words on a $3/4$-inch round self-adhesive dot that fits on top of a crown cap or over a cork; I tend to put the date and type of mead on the label. Using your computer and printer, you can easily print up labels to stick on the side of each bottle. Your imagination is the limit on how fancy you want to make the labels. Since I tend to reuse bottles, I don't want to make the labels too hard to remove. So I use a child-safe glue stick on the back of the label. The glue holds but is water-soluble.

A simple stovetop water bath like this a good way to create colorful wax seals for swing-top bottles.

KEGGING

The kegs used by homebrewers are typically called corny kegs. These kegs get their name from one of their major producers, the IMI Cornelius Company. They were once the mainstay of the soft drink industry, but have since been pretty much eliminated. They normally have a small oval lid with two connections next to it, one for pushing gas into the keg and the other for removing liquid from the keg, a connection that has a long tube to the bottom. The beverages inside these kegs come in contact only with stainless steel.

Of the two major variants of kegs available, the first is known as the pin-lock style because the connectors on the keg have little protruding pins keyed so that you cannot insert a fitting onto the incorrect position. The connections are locked in place by a slight twist of the mating connector over the protruding pins. The other variant is known as the ball-lock style because small stainless ball bearings lock the fittings in place. Historically, Pepsi-Cola used the ball-lock style kegs and Coca-Cola used the pin-lock style kegs, but both styles work fine for beer, wine, and mead. The styles have minor variations relating to handles and base material, but as long as the keg will hold pressure, it will work.

For the 5-gallon (19-liter) keg size (the most common size for both the ball-lock and pin-lock styles), the two styles do have slightly different dimensions for the same volume. Alternative sizes include a 3-gallon (11-liter) size and a 10-gallon (38-liter) size. Both of these sizes are rare, and used versions of both styles of kegs are becoming difficult to find.

The full keg setup requires a number of other components as well, including a gas cylinder, a corresponding gas pressure regulator, quick disconnects for both the liquid and gas fitting for your type of keg, some sort of tap (the faucet for dispensing the mead), a few feet of high-pressure gas hose, and finally a few feet of beverage hose to connect the tap up. The regulator and the gas cylinder have to be a matched set. Different gas choices require different cylinders and types of valves, and the regulator has to mate with the valve.

A true, intentional sparkling mead (like beer and soda) fizzes as carbon dioxide comes out of solution. However, a normal keg works by applying gas pressure to the "gas in" connector and removing the mead via the "liquid out" connector, but leaving carbon dioxide pressure on a keg will eventually result in carbonation, even if that wasn't planned. Unfortunately, most corny kegs require at least a little gas pressure to maintain a reliable seal; the seal keeps air and other contaminants out. For home beer- and meadmakers, by far the most common gas cylinder is for carbon dioxide (CO_2), but if you really want a still mead to come out of your keg, you need to use a gas, such as nitrogen, to push the mead that doesn't readily dissolve. Nitrogen is readily available and safe, and you can use pure nitrogen or a mixture of nitrogen and carbon dioxide called "beer gas" or "Guinness gas" in the industry. Beer gas will still slowly cause a slight carbonation of your mead, but since the majority of the gas is nitrogen, the carbonation level will be much less than with pure carbon dioxide. Both pure nitrogen and beer gas use the same cylinder and regulator, so you can switch without any equipment change. You can also use argon, an inert gas that does not readily dissolve in mead.

Using kegs makes carbonating your mead really easy. Carbonation levels are typically measured in volumes of carbon dioxide, where one volume means there is as much gaseous carbon dioxide as liquid in the mead. For reference when selecting a carbonation level: American light lagers are typically 2.5–2.8 volumes; sodas are typically 3.0–4.2 volumes; and champagne is typically 5–6 volumes. Referring to a standard chart of pressure versus temperature will allow you to dial in the exact carbonation level you desire. A few days of holding the pressure, and the proper setting will result in the carbonation level you selected.

If you plan to use kegs for your mead and want to set up the kind of metal taps you see in a bar for serving beer, you need to be extra careful. The cheaper metal tap parts are usually made of chrome- or nickel-plated brass. Unfortunately, meads can have a fairly low (acidic) pH level that can slowly eat the chrome or nickel plating, and then the mead will be exposed to brass, creating a metallic taste in your great mead. If you want to set up a tap system to serve mead, go with stainless steel for the metal parts that will come in contact with the mead.

Once you have your mead in a keg, it can be pretty easy to fill a few bottles when you want to take some with you or when you want to enter a competition. You just sanitize the bottles, caps, and serving tap setup, then run mead into the bottle and cap the bottle. Bottling a sparkling mead can be a little more complicated, however, because the carbonated mead will start fizzing and make it hard to get the cap on fast enough to actually have a full bottle. Chilling the mead as close to freezing as possible will help, but the process can still be difficult. Fortunately, the homemade beer industry has developed several gadgets to make bottling sparkling meads easier. Counter-pressure fillers connect to the "liquid out" fitting of the corny keg and to the gas regulator and allow you to purge a bottle with gas carbon dioxide first and then fill the bottle to the proper level.

Kegs also make it fairly easy to use a filter to clarify a mead. A filter can be attached between a keg full of mead and another empty, sanitized keg, and then gas pressure from the regulator can be used to force the mead through the filter. A number of different grades of filters are available. They're rated by how small of a particle the filter will remove. I have only extremely rarely found it necessary to filter a mead, but filtering does offer a nice option if you cannot get a mead to clarify by other means.

Kegging is, of course, another option for packaging your mead. The kegs used by homebrewers are typically called corny kegs. They get their name from one of their major producers, the IMI Cornelius Company.

8 ADVANCED TECHNIQUES

TINCTURES

Tinctures are concentrated solutions of the essential characteristics of an ingredient used to increase those characteristics in a mead. A tincture can be made with water, mead, or alcohol added to a simple syrup base created by boiling sugar or honey in water, a common practice in mixing cocktails. Tinctures work for a diverse range of ingredients, from wood to spices to flowers to fruits.

Tinctures are easiest to make in a glass vessel like a canning jar with a tightly sealing lid. A swing-top beer bottle will work for items that will fit through the neck. When using water or mead as the liquid, sanitation is essential. For water, boiled is best, but using vodka or stronger distilled spirits avoids the sanitation concerns all together. The different solvents can yield different results, and some characteristics may be more soluble in one solvent than the others. Heat can also affect the extraction process, and oxidation can be a concern with tinctures, particularly when using mead as the base liquid. For tinctures with a mead base, be sure that the jar is filled to the top to minimize air space.

Since you want the tincture to have strong characteristics of an ingredient, you want to put a lot of it into the jar, enough to adjust an entire batch of mead. If you're starting with a mead base, ingredients that add water or sugar may restart the fermentation of your tincture if fermentation stopped because the yeast reached its alcohol tolerance level. For example, this could happen when creating a tincture with fruit. Adding a tincture that contains fermentable sugars to a finished mead may also restart a fermentation.

For most ingredients, a few days to weeks in the jar will extract most or all of the characteristics you are going to get. Tinctures extracted with distilled spirits tend to be stable and can be stored in sealed containers for a long time, but water or simple syrup–style tinctures may only last for a few weeks, although refrigeration helps extend shelf life a little.

BLENDING

Some home beer- and winemakers seem to think blending is cheating, that you should be able to make exactly the target beverage right from the start. Perhaps they can, but I blend as necessary.

WHY BLEND?

Blending two meads can create a beverage that is better than either in isolation. The melding of the characteristics can be better than a sum of its parts. Blending can be used to adjust alcohol levels, residual sugar levels, acid levels, color, flavor, and aroma. It can even be used as a means of stopping fermentation, which really is just blending to get the alcohol level above the yeast's alcohol tolerance. I find blending a dry mead with a sweeter version with the same or similar ingredients results in a softer, more pleasant character than back-sweetening with raw honey does.

Beware of causing renewed fermentation by lowering the alcohol level below the yeast's tolerance or by giving the yeast more sugar before the mead reaches the yeast's alcohol tolerance. You can prevent renewed fermentation in several ways: first, by keeping the mead cold (refrigerated) after blending; second, by stabilizing the mead with potassium sorbate before blending (Chapter 8); and third, by pasteurizing the mead.

THE SCIENCE PART

Blending is easier when you start with a desired characteristic that can be measured and blend two different batches with different values of that characteristic to achieve a target value. Pearson's square can help you visualize blending two items to adjust measurable things like specific gravity or alcohol level, but it doesn't apply for subjective blending of things like flavor or aroma. The technique only works when one input is below the target value and the other is above it. For example, say you have the following inputs: a mead with 14 percent alcohol (B) that you want to raise to 20 percent (T) by blending with some distilled spirits that have 90 percent alcohol (A). You can compute the ratio for blending as D = T − B and E = A − T. In other words the resulting values D = 6 and E = 70.

Pearson's Square

A = high concentration
B = low concentration
T = target concentration
D = parts of high concentration
E = parts of low concentration
D = T − B
E = A − T

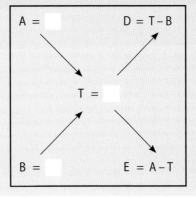

$$A = \boxed{} \qquad D = T - B$$
$$T = \boxed{}$$
$$B = \boxed{} \qquad E = A - T$$

That means we need 6 parts of the distilled spirits at 90 percent for 70 parts of the mead at 14 percent, and the result will be 76 parts of mead at 20 percent.

As another example, you have a mead that is at 1.050 and another mead that is at 1.000 and you want to blend to get a mead at 1.012. You have: A = 1.050, B =1.000, and T = 1.012, resulting in D = 0.012 and E = 0.038. In this case, using specific gravity gives you a little more work; you multiply D and E by 1000 to rationalize the numbers and then blend 12 parts of the 1.050 mead with 38 parts of the 1.000 mead to get 50 parts of 1.012 mead.

THE CRAFT PART

Blending for flavor and aroma is really a craft and not a science. As you increase your experience with it, you can get better at it. Asking several different people to evaluate the blend can help you rule out individual palate differences, weaknesses, and even bias (if you prepare the blend, it can bias your perceptions).

You can blend to modify the flavor and/or aroma, to modify the color, to modify the acidity, to modify the alcohol level, to increase complexity, and to adjust the sweetness. Blending is the only way to easily reduce the wood character if you used too much—same for reducing the spice levels if you used too much.

If you have a mead that suffers from some process flaws, blending may not rescue the bad mead but may just result in a larger quantity of mediocre mead. Process flaws would include things like improper sanitation (resulting in improper flavors or aromas from contamination) and excessive oxidation.

Always start your blending with a trial on a small scale. When blending, you generally want to minimize oxidation, so avoid splashing or excessive stirring. Beware that sometimes the blend may not stand up with time because the characteristics continue to meld after they are blended; even a few weeks of aging can change the perception of the blend. If you're blending for immediate consumption, that won't be a problem, but long-term storage can change the results.

Always make sure the meads you are blending have completely finished fermenting and are stable. If they are not both fermented to the yeast's alcohol tolerance, then you may need to treat them with potassium sorbate or otherwise make sure that fermentation does not restart after blending.

ROUGH CUTS

The idea of a rough cut is to get close to the proper blend and then to hone in on the final ratio in subsequent trials. You don't need to be blending two different meads; you could be blending a mead and a wine, a mead and a beer, or even mead and distilled spirits. The techniques are the same.

For this process, you'll initially produce four different glasses of the blend, each at a different ratio of the two items being combined. To minimize unwanted bias effects, use the same type of glass (shape, size, and color) for all the blends. Each glass will get a total of 20 parts of mead. A part can be as simple as 1 tablespoon (5 milliliters); just make sure it is the same throughout the blending session. In the table, A represents the first mead and B represents the second mead. The rough-cut blends will change by 20 percent (4 parts in 20) per step. You will also need a glass that contains only mead A and another with just mead B. Label the glasses before pouring the appropriate parts of each mead in and stirring to mix. A small piece of paper under the glass can serve as the label, or a grease pencil can be used to mark the glass.

Rough-Cut Blend Ratios			
Label	A% : B%	Parts of A	Parts of B
1	100 : 0	20	0
5	80 : 20	16	4
9	60 : 40	12	8
13	40 : 60	8	12
17	20 : 80	4	16
21	0 : 100	0	20

Now start tasting and smelling the blends. You want to select the glass that has a little too much of the dominant character and then the glass that has the next-lower amount of that character. For example, if the A mead has the dominant character, and you found sample 9 to have a little too much of A, then you would select samples 9 and 5. Set these samples aside and proceed to fine-tune.

FINE-TUNING

You have now selected the two coarse endpoints you need to fine-tune the blend. This time you will adjust by 5 percent (1 part in 20) per sample. The table shows all the different finer blends, but you only need to prepare the three that are between the two you selected in the rough cut; the samples produced as rough cuts are bolded in the table. In the example above, the rough cuts were samples 9 and 5, so we need to produce blends for 6, 7, and 8. Be sure to label each blend correctly.

Fine-Tune Blend Ratios			
Label	**A% : B%**	**Parts of A**	**Parts of B**
1	**100 : 0**	**20**	**0**
2	95 : 5	19	1
3	90 : 10	18	2
4	85 : 15	17	3
5	**80 : 20**	**16**	**4**
6	75 : 25	15	5
7	70 : 30	14	6
8	65 : 35	13	7
9	**60 : 40**	**12**	**8**
10	55 : 45	11	9
11	50 : 50	10	10
12	45 : 55	9	11
13	**40 : 60**	**8**	**12**
14	35 : 65	7	13
15	30 : 70	6	14
16	25 : 75	5	15
17	**20 : 80**	**4**	**16**
18	15 : 85	3	17
19	10 : 90	2	18
20	5 : 95	1	19
21	**0 : 100**	**0**	**20**

Using the five glasses, two selected from the rough cut and three fining blends between those endpoints, select the single trial that seems best. While you could then extend the technique further and produce another set of blends with a one percent step between samples, you are looking at diminishing returns, as most people may not be able to perceive those small changes. If you have time, you can prepare a single bottle of the selected blend ratio and let it age for a few weeks before reevaluating the blend to see if the characteristics have changed as they melded during aging.

Once you have the final ratio, you can proceed to blending a bigger (or the entire) quantity and then finish and package the mead.

AGING

While a fair amount has been written about aging wines, there is little about aging meads. White wines are lower in tannins and other phenols than red wines, so red wines tend to survive aging better than white wines. However, some white wines with a higher acid level also seem to age better than other white wines. White wines aged in wood pick up phenols from the wood that improve the aging potential.

The acidity of wines and meads may change during aging due to the esterification of the acids, or the combining of alcohols and acids to form esters. These esters make the mead or wine more fruity. During aging the phenolic compounds will start to aggregate, and eventually some will settle out, resulting in a reduction of the tannin levels and even a change in color. If the mead was not cold-conditioned earlier, aging can result in the formation of tartate crystals as some of the tartaric acid is eliminated from the mead. These transformations can change the balance of your mead over time.

Some generalization from wines to meads seems reasonable. Pure honey has virtually no phenols and no tannins, so extending the wine generalities to mead indicates that straight meads low in acid are not going to have much aging potential, while those with more acidity can last longer. Melomels made with fruits containing phenols or tannins, pyments made with red grape varieties, and many metheglins are going to have more phenols than straight meads and thus will have the potential to age well. Pyments made with white wine grapes that are fairly acidic will tend to last better than nonacidic varieties.

Remember that aging potential does not mean the mead (or wine) won't change over time. It really just means the beverage will continue to be drinkable over time.

Just as for wine, aging conditions can significantly impact the results. Vibrations and temperature variations will accelerate deterioration. For example, cycling a mead back and forth from a refrigerator to room temperature a few times can hasten its demise. Storage near vibrating machines like washing machines, dryers, and fans is bad. Exposure to sunlight can accelerate oxidation. In general, the rate of the chemical reactions doubles for each 18°F (10°C) temperature increase. Wine experts recommend storage at a nominal cellar temperature of 55°F (13°C). In my house, the basement varies from about 58°F (14°C) in deep winter to about 70°F (21°C) at the end of summer. I do, however, have the ability to store a few kegs of mead at about 36°F (2°C) to extend their life.

The two types of aging, oxidative and reductive, are named for the primary chemical transformations that happen during each. Oxidative aging occurs in the presence of oxygen. A small amount of oxygen gets into unsealed containers when the mead is racked or even when the airlock and stopper are removed for sampling. Reductive aging only starts once the mead is packaged in a sealed container that allows no more oxygen to be introduced.

In the wine world, reductive wines would typically be white or rosé wines with fresh fruity characteristics. They can be lower in alcohol, higher in acid, and lower in tannin and can have more residual sweetness. They are intended to be served fairly quickly, in part to minimize oxidation.

Oxidative wines are allowed to take up small amounts of oxygen during aging, which will continue to alter the characteristics of the wine. These wines will have more alcohol and more tannin as they enter into the oxidation reactions during aging. Barrel aging will facilitate oxidative processes, and long aging in corked bottles will allow slow oxidation. Wines that benefit from oxidative aging are reds such as Bordeaux and Burgundy, as well as sherries and Portuguese ports.

Both forms of aging can be extended to meads. The fresh fruity meads (straight meads, light-colored melomels, and some white grape pyments) parallel the wines that are reductive. They tend to do better when consumed fairly young (in a few years). The more tannic and bigger meads, such as dark melomels, red grape pyments, and metheglins high in tannins, will do well with oxidative aging.

IN GLASS

Aging in a carboy involves bulk aging and oxidative aging. In the wine world, a few months of bulk aging for white wines up to as much as a few years for some red wines is acceptable. The process of getting the mead out of the carboy and into the final package is going to introduce some oxygen and result in bottle shock. Generally, after bottling, a few weeks will be needed to fully incorporate the oxygen into the mead; until this happens, the mead may taste different than it did before bottling. Packaging ends the oxidative aging as the final oxygen is incorporated and the reductive aging begins.

In the wine world, wines packaged in larger bottles seem to age more slowly than wine in the standard 750-milliliter bottle, probably because less air is introduced during bottling. Bottling with systems that introduce neutral gases (carbon dioxide, argon, or even nitrogen) into the bottle rather than air further improves the mead's aging potential.

The rules governing the aging of wine don't generalize to bottle-conditioned sparkling meads, however. Virtually all wine is bottled with no sediment, but a bottle-conditioned mead is going to have sediment that contains the live yeast used for carbonation. The aging of bottle-conditioned mead will be more like that of bottle-conditioned beer; the live yeast in the bottle will quickly consume any oxygen introduced during bottling. Bottle-conditioned beers tend to have much better aging potential than the same beer packaged without the yeast, but you definitely want to avoid warm temperatures after the yeast has completed carbonating the bottle. Bottle-conditioned meads are pretty rare but have great potential for long-term storage.

IN WOOD

Oxidative aging in a wooden barrel involves a slow ingress of oxygen through the wood and the bung opening. However, some of the oxygen intake will be offset by complex phenols the mead takes up from the wood. Further, some liquid will be lost to evaporation; in the whiskey world, they call the lost portion the angel's share. Generally, long-term aging in wood is not a good idea.

If you are bottling a mead that you want to last for a long time, here are a couple of techniques to minimize the gradual uptake of oxygen into the bottle: first, insert a wine cork flush into the bottle and then a crown cap over the cork; and second (can be combined with the first), dip the top of the capped bottle into some molten wax.

ICING (EISING)

Icing a mead is similar to the process used for a traditional German icebock. After fermentation has completed and the mead is ready for packaging, you need to freeze it—not frozen solid, just to the slushy stage. At that point you want to extract the still-liquid part and leave the slush behind. Alternatively, you could freeze the mead solid and then just collect the first portion that melts. A typical target is to remove 10–20 percent of the original volume as slush or ice. When done properly, the slush removed does not have much flavor or alcohol in it, which results in a significant increase in the alcohol content of the mead.

Icing a mead is not going to improve a mediocre mead. Water will form the bulk of what you leave behind in the slush, but a few other compounds may precipitate as you freeze the mead. I find that icing a mead can really improve the aroma and flavors, softening the rough edges of the initial mead.

You can experiment with icing on a small scale by putting some mead in a sanitized plastic jug or bottle and then placing it in your freezer. Once it's slushy, you can pour the mead through a sanitized strainer to collect the result. You may find that the freezer compartment of your refrigerator does not get cold enough to freeze some high-alcohol, relatively sweet meads. Also, I try not to fill the plastic jugs over two-thirds full to avoid making a mess in the freezer as the mead expands while freezing. Icing a sparkling mead will remove some carbonation, but some will last through the process.

GETTING A SWEETER MEAD

You will make meads that you really wish had finished sweeter. It can be difficult to create a sweet mead if you aren't sure when the yeast has reached its alcohol tolerance level; the mead may appear sweet for a while, but the yeast may have just slowed down its fermentation rate. For example, given that most yeast strains available to meadmakers are able to tolerate from 11 percent to 18 percent ABV, it is hard to make a hydromel that doesn't finish very dry without resorting to post-fermentation sweetening of the mead. A yeast with 11 percent ABV tolerance can ferment away about 83 specific gravity points, which means it can take a mead from 1.083 to 1.000. A 14 percent ABV–tolerant yeast can take a 1.105 specific gravity mead to about 1.000.

You can safely sweeten a mead post-fermentation using several techniques, but just adding more honey isn't going to work if the yeast hasn't reached its alcohol tolerance level. Potassium sorbate and chilling will not completely stop the yeast but rather try to minimize additional activity. Pasteurization, however, will truly stop further fermentation.

POTASSIUM SORBATE ADDITION TO STOP RENEWED FERMENTATION

First, a common misconception seems to be that potassium sorbate stops further fermentations. This is *not true*. Potassium sorbate additions keep the existing yeast cells from reproducing but do not keep existing cells from continuing to ferment sugar into alcohol. While potassium sorbate is generally effective against *Saccharomyces* yeasts strains, it does not inhibit spoilage organisms like lactic acid bacteria and *Brettanomyces*.

Potassium sorbate is a salt of sorbic acid, so adding potassium sorbate means you're adding sorbic acid to your mead, making it taste very slightly acidic. Some people even perceive sorbic acid as a rancid character. Before using sorbate, you need to minimize the number of yeast cells in the mead, at minimum by racking off all the sediment. Filtering the mead is even better.

Since sorbic acid is not effective against all spoilage bacteria, you need to treat the mead with some potassium metabisulfite to add some sulfites (sulfur dioxide) that will control the spoilage organisms. Lactic bacteria are a major concern when using potassium sorbate, because they can metabolize sorbic acid into the characteristic of crushed geranium leaves (2-ethoxyhexa-3,5-diene). You should never use sorbate in a mead that has undergone or is going to undergo malolactic fermentation (used to reduce acidity); it will eventually end up tasting like crushed geranium leaves.

Potassium sorbate additions are not stable long-term; the resulting sorbic acid breaks down to ethyl sorbate that has notes of candied or artificial fruit, Juicy Fruit gum, celery, and pineapple. Ethyl sorbate will build up over time as more sorbic acid breaks down, so potassium sorbate treatment isn't appropriate for meads you intend to age. The time it takes for sorbic acid to become ethyl sorbate depends on a number of factors, including temperature, pH, alcohol level, and others, but will typically happen within 6 to 12 months.

The amount of potassium sorbate needed to treat a mead decreases as the alcohol level goes up; alcohol also inhibits the yeast. Since the density (weight-to-volume ratio) for potassium sorbate varies, you should follow the label instructions but aim a little high rather than lower for your dose. You need the sulfite level to be at least 40 ppm (measure with a Titret SO_2 kit); add potassium metabisulfite if necessary. Remember, the sulfur dioxide is necessary to avoid the geranium characteristics.

Sorbate may introduce some floaters in a mead that was previously clear, but waiting at least 24 hours before bottling will allow some of them to settle out. If you are going to cold-condition the mead, do so after adding the sorbate.

CHILLING TO STOP FERMENTATION EARLY

Cold conditions significantly reduce the activity of yeasts. If you can keep your mead cold, you can stop the fermentation when the desired sweetness is reached. Just keep sampling the mead while fermentation is underway and rapidly chill it once you reach the desired sweetness level. The colder you can get it without freezing it solid, the better. However, the resulting mead is not stable; if the mead is warmed up, there is a good chance it will start to ferment again. You can stabilize the product if you have the equipment to sterile-filter the mead once it is chilled, or you can treat it with potassium sorbate or pasteurize it.

PASTEURIZATION TO STOP FERMENTATION EARLY

Pasteurization is a conceptually simple process common in commercial food production, but home beer-, wine-, and meadmakers rarely use it. The process involves either increasing temperature or increasing time of exposure to a particular temperature. One pasteurization unit equals holding the liquid at 140°F (60°C) for 1 minute.

Pasteurization stops fermentation by killing all or nearly all the yeast, and it may cause a slight degradation of the flavors and aromas. If pectin remains in the mead, pasteurization may also cause a slight haze.

The pasteurization process can be used for sweet, sparkling meads that are bottle-conditioned. You will need to periodically monitor the mead to see when sufficient carbonation has developed in the bottles and then stop the fermentation, leaving a sweet but sparkling mead that won't become overcarbonated.

The big problem at the home level lies in getting the mead to the appropriate temperature and then back down to storage temperature. While the mead only needs to be at 140°F (60°C) for a couple of minutes, it will take a long time to heat and cool it. If you want to try the technique, you need to start with strong bottles; I suggest using returnable-style beer bottles or champagne bottles, as they are more likely to survive the thermal shock produced in the process. Use a hot water bath in a large pot with a cover. Also, for consistent results, use identical bottles so the timing is the same for all of them.

Heat water to 190–200°F (88–93°C) and then place some of the filled bottles in the hot water and cover the pot. You will need to have one bottle open and insert a thermometer into it. When the thermometer says the mead in the bottle has reached 140°F (60°C), wait a couple of minutes and then remove the bottles and place them in a pot of cool (not cold) water to return them to storage temperature. The process depends on the water being able to heat the contents of the bottles to 140°F (60°C); you will need to heat only a few bottles at a time for that to work.

It is hard to predict exact time requirements for home pasteurization, since the size of the pot, the hot water temperature, the weight of the bottles, the initial temperature of the bottles, the temperature of the cold bath, and other factors all influence the process. However, after you try it on a few bottles, you can set up a repeatable system using your equipment.

YEAST CHOICE

The different yeast strains (see Chapter 4) have important differences, such as alcohol tolerance, oxygen needs, fermentation temperature range, and nutrient needs, along with differing aroma and flavor profiles. Some strains may be traditionally associated with certain types of wines and therefore would be a reasonable choice for a pyment using the same grape.

As you expand your yeast horizons, don't be limited to mead or even wine strains; looking at the descriptions of the various strains available to beer-makers may give you some new ideas on how to get a desired characteristic into your mead.

CONTROLLING PH DURING FERMENTATION

Fermentation will naturally increase the acidity of the must or mead as it progresses. Most mead fermentations are going to work best in the 3.4–4 pH range. My meads get there without any adjustment. My tap water is very high in calcium and carbonates, so it naturally has buffers that help keep the fermentation from getting too acidic.

If you need to adjust the must to a higher (more neutral) pH, potassium carbonate is a good choice, but if you can't find potassium carbonate, calcium carbonate (chalk) is readily available in homebrew supply stores, although it doesn't dissolve in water easily. I've also seen discussions about using potassium hydroxide (KOH) to increase the pH, but I haven't needed that technique with my water. KOH is a strong base, so you should first create a concentrated solution of KOH and then only add a very small amount at a time to the must to make your adjustment.

SIDE-BY-SIDE EXPERIMENTS

Side-by-side experiments, in which you mix up a batch of must and then split the fermentation into two or more different fermenters that are handled differently, allow you to compare outcomes. You'll need to keep much of the process and ingredients common between the fermenters to get a good comparison. It's a little harder to control the amount of stirring in each fermenter during side-by-side fermentations, but using a timer and the same drill and stirring wand may help you get consistency.

Yeast comparisons are an obvious choice, and fermentation temperature experiments using the same yeast can be enlightening. Adjusting the nutrient dose and/or time of addition can help you learn about the performance of a yeast strain. Experiments related to time of introduction of ingredients can help you hone a flavor you are looking to enhance or reduce.

No matter what you want to investigate, it is best to minimize the things you change between the comparison batches; too many changes make it hard to really isolate the cause.

NON-*SACCHAROMYCES* FERMENTATION

To really get into the advanced fermentation of meads, you can consider fermenting your mead with something other than *Saccharomyces* (or members of the yeast family). Most mead, wine, and beer yeasts are either *S. cerevisiae* or *S. bayanus*, but craft brewers have shown a lot of interest in using *Brettanomyces (Brett)* either in combination with *Saccharomyces* or in a pure *Brettanomyces* fermentation. See Chapter 4 for more on *Brettanomyces*.

A very unusual mead, traditional Ethiopian t'ej is spontaneously fermented. The ingredients are very basic: honey, water, and either *gesho inchet* (dried twigs from the gesho plant) or *gesho kitel* (dried leaves from the gesho plant). Some descriptions call the gesho plant hops, but they are not related to the type of hops used in beer. The organisms that ferment the mead are found on the gesho plant.

9 RECIPE DEVELOPMENT

RECIPE DEVELOPMENT IS PART ART AND PART SCIENCE. The science relates to selecting a handful of numerical parameters for your mead recipe: things like the batch size, the original gravity, the final gravity, and the alcohol level. The art refers to choosing the yeast strain, the honey, and the special ingredients and getting or adjusting to the final balance you desire.

WHAT DO YOU WANT TO MAKE?

The first step in developing a recipe is deciding what you want to make. Do you want a dry mead, a sweet mead, or somewhere in between? Do you want high alcohol, low alcohol, or something in the middle? Are you looking to showcase a special honey in the mead? Will it be a straight honey mead or will other ingredients be used? Are there any special fruits, spices, or other ingredients you want to showcase, and will they be subtle or obvious?

PARAMETERS

Some interdependence exists in the numerical aspects of a mead. The combination of the original gravity and final gravity determine the alcohol level in the mead, and you can control at most two of those three numbers for a particular batch. The approximate alcohol content can be calculated from the difference between the original gravity and the final gravity.

$$ABV = 131 * (OG - FG)$$

For example, with an OG of 1.115 and a FG of 1.005, the ABV would be approximately 14.4 percent.

$$ABV = 14.41 = 131 * (1.115 - 1.005)$$

While back-sweetening after fermentation will increase the apparent final gravity, it will also increase the apparent original gravity and will not significantly change the alcohol level, unless the back sweetening restarts fermentation.

BATCH SIZE

Your batch size will be determined mainly by your equipment. You don't want to target a size bigger than your carboy(s). During bulk aging in the carboy you want to minimize air space, so starting your batch size just a little larger than your carboy size will allow for a small loss during racking and will still fill your containers to the top. Since typical carboys or jugs come in 1-, 3-, 5-, 6-, and 7-gallon (4-, 12-, 19-, 23-, and 27-liter) sizes, those are good target sizes to choose, but you can decide to make your batch size big enough to fill several carboys for aging.

You may want to make a fairly small batch if you are experimenting with unusual ingredients or if you have a limited supply of an ingredient. For example, if you could obtain only 10 pounds (4.53 kilograms) of black currants and want to use 3 pounds (1.36 kilograms) per gallon (3.79 liters) of mead, you make a 3.3-gallon (12.5-liter) batch intending to age it in a 3-gallon (12-liter) carboy.

My primary fermenters are plastic, either 6-gallon (23-liter) buckets or 12-gallon (45-liter) plastic bins. I find filling the primary fermenter no more than one-half to two-thirds full leaves sufficient space for the foam created during the periodic stirring.

If you measure your carboy, you are likely to find it holds a little more than the advertised volume. For example, my 6.5-gallon (24.6-liter) acid carboys hold a tad over 7 gallons (26.5 liters). Measuring will allow you to target your batch size to minimize air space in the carboy.

TARGETING ORIGINAL GRAVITY

The original gravity will determine if the mead is a hydromel, standard-strength, or sack-strength mead. (See the section about strength in Chapter 2.) Further, the target original gravity and the batch size determine how much fermentable sugar will be in the mead. While a sack-strength mead will have lots of complexity, it will also have lots of alcohol, meaning you won't be able to drink much of it at a time. Even the typical hydromel is going to be stronger than the typical beer, ranging as high as 7.5 percent ABV. A hydromel makes a lighter mead that can be more approachable to most people.

As I mentioned before, fruit contains about 85 percent water by weight, and since water weighs 8.33 pounds (3.78 kilograms) per gallon on average, adding 9.8 pounds (4.45 kilograms) of fruit is like adding 1 gallon (3.79 liters) of water to the mead but very little sugar. (See the fruit section in Chapter 3.) That means that adding fruit to a must that was at your target OG actually reduces the effective OG. Knowing how much fruit you plan to add to the mead allows you to adjust the original gravity before the fruit addition to get your target original gravity. It will also allow you to calculate the batch size before the fruit addition.

Targeting Original Gravity

$$TOG = \text{target original gravity}$$
$$FW = \text{fruit weight}$$
$$FWP = \text{fruit water percent}$$
$$FSP = \text{fruit sugar percent}$$
$$BS = \text{batch size}$$
$$NS = \text{size before fruit addition}$$
$$BOG = \text{before fruit original gravity}$$
$$FS = \text{sugar from fruit}$$
$$NS = BS - (FWP \times FW)/8.33$$
$$FS = FSP \times FW \times 46$$
$$BOG = 1 + \left(\dfrac{\dfrac{(BS \times (TOG - 1) \times 1000) - FS}{NS}}{1000} \right)$$

Using sample values of a target OG of 1.115, 12 pounds (5.44 kilograms) of fruit that is 86 percent water and 6 percent sugar, and a batch size of 5 gallons (19 liters):

$$TOG = 1.115$$
$$FW = 12$$
$$FWP = .86$$
$$FSP = .06$$
$$BS = 5$$

The equations show:

$$NS = 5 - (.86 \times 12)/8.33 = 3.76$$
$$FS = .06 \times 12 \times 46 = 33.12$$

$$BOG = 1 + \cfrac{\left(\cfrac{((5 \times (1.115 - 1) \times 1000) - 33.12)}{3.76} \right)}{1000} = 1.144$$

This means the batch size before the fruit addition should be 3.76 gallons (14.23 liters), and the original gravity before the fruit addition needs to be 1.144. This will create 5 gallons (19 liters) of must with an original gravity of 1.115 after the fruit is added. Note that you won't be able to read that 1.115 on your hydrometer, because the fruit won't release the water right away. So when mixing up the must you need to make only 3.76 gallons (14.23 liters) at OG 1.144 to compensate for the water and sugar derived from the fruit. You may want to bump the batch size a quart or two (a liter or two) to account for the fruit pulp that will be left behind when you rack the mead off the fruit and into a carboy.

The original gravity (or the before-fruit original gravity) chart below will help you determine how many pounds of honey per gallon of must you will need. The horizontal lines show the approximate alcohol level (5 percent, 10 percent, and 15 percent) with an average yeast strain if the mead is fermented down to 1.000 FG.

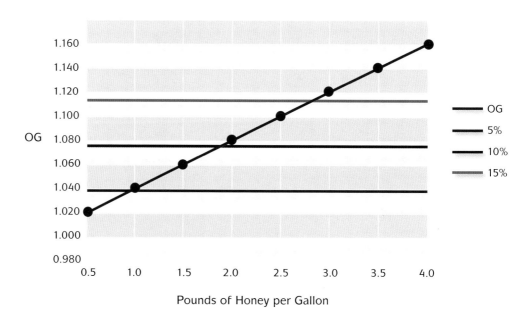

Mead Strength

TARGETING FINAL GRAVITY

If the original gravity is sufficient, the final gravity and alcohol level will be determined by the yeast's alcohol limit. In the following table, if the original gravity is as shown and the final gravity is 1.000, the alcohol by volume of mead will be as indicated. Using the alcohol tolerance for your yeast strain and the original gravity of your mead will allow you to determine if the yeast will reach its alcohol tolerance.

Targeting Final Gravity	
ABV	SG
5	1.038
6	1.046
7	1.053
8	1.061
9	1.069
10	1.076
11	1.084
12	1.092
13	1.099
14	1.107
15	1.115
16	1.122
17	1.130
18	1.137
19	1.145
20	1.153

Unless you use techniques to arrest the fermentation before the yeast reaches its limits, the way to control the final gravity is by targeting an original gravity (equivalent to the yeast's limit) above the desired final gravity. For example, if you want a final gravity of 1.015 and you are using a yeast with an alcohol limit of 12 percent (1.092 from the table above), you need to target an OG of 1.107:

$$YT = \text{yeast tolerance} = 1.092$$
$$OG = 1 + (FG - 1) + (YT - 1)$$
$$OG = 1 + (1.092 - 1) + (1.015 - 1) = 1.107$$

If the original gravity is less than the yeast's limit, the mead will ferment to a dry level, a final gravity around or even below 1.000. Alternatively, if you use the techniques for getting a sweeter mead in Chapter 8, you can arrest the fermentation before the yeast reaches its limit or you can adjust the final gravity post-fermentation.

YEAST SELECTION

The major criteria for selecting the yeast strain for your mead are:

- Aroma and flavor characteristics
- Nutrient requirements
- Temperature tolerance
- Alcohol tolerance
- Fermentation performance (flocculation, foam production, and so on)

I typically make my strain choices based mainly on the aroma or flavor characteristics and then on the alcohol tolerance. When making a pyment with an identifiable grape variety, I may choose a wine yeast typically used for that grape variety. The yeast strain description might mention a flavor or aroma nuance that strikes you as appropriate for some of the special ingredients in your recipe. My go-to yeast if nothing strikes me as special for the mead I'm making is Narbonne (Lalvin 71B-1122).

Looking at the yeast strain descriptions (Chapter 4), the wine and mead strains range from 11 to 18 percent in alcohol tolerance, with the typical beer strains ranging from 8 percent and up. If you want a mead that finishes with an alcohol level below 11 percent, you are going to have to be creative in finding a yeast, or you will have to use the techniques in Chapter 8 to stop fermentation early.

HONEY CHOICE

Some selection criteria for honey include:

- Aroma or flavor needs to reinforce other ingredients.
- Aroma or flavor needs to contrast other ingredients.
- Plays only a supporting role (so any mild honey is acceptable).
- Varietal honey character needs to dominate.
- Complex (but indistinct) honey character is desired.
- The honey is locally available.

Looking at the honey descriptions in Chapter 3 will help you determine whether the aroma and/or flavor of a honey may meld well with the other ingredients in a mead. For example, the woody aspects of tupelo honey work well with Chardonnay grape juice; many people like Chardonnay wine that has a woody (oaky) character. Clover honey is mild and easily overpowered by other ingredients. A blend of several honey varieties or a wildflower honey will result in an indistinct honey character that is still complex. A locally available honey can be a good choice for many meads; honey is heavy and therefore expensive to ship from distant locations.

SPECIAL INGREDIENTS SELECTION

Selecting special ingredients, the things beyond the honey, water, yeast, and nutrients that will go into your mead, is an art. The creative space is wide, but not all ingredients and combinations will appeal to everyone. Your special ingredients can range from subtle to dominant in the mead.

When using fruits in your mead, remember that sweetness tends to reinforce the fruit character. While not an absolute requirement, I find some fruits, like melons, need some residual sweetness for people to perceive the fruit. Apricot tends to have a faint character, so adding some peaches brings out the apricot character.

COMBINATIONS OF INGREDIENTS

The single-fruit melomel or the single-spice metheglin can be exciting, but don't feel you need to stay with just a single ingredient. Combinations can be more than the sum of the parts. Look for combinations that meld for increased complexity or that contrast each other. Examples include:

- Cherries and vanilla
- Apples and cinnamon (and perhaps some nutmeg)
- Peaches and mace
- Raspberries and hot peppers
- Citrus and ginger
- Peaches and mangoes
- Tart cherries, currants, and raspberries
- Strawberries and bananas
- Raspberries and chocolate (with or without hot peppers)
- Hot peppers and smoke

Don't feel the need to stick to single ingredients for your melomels and metheglins. Combinations can be more than the sum of their parts.

Juice combinations in the grocery store and modern cocktail recipes are a good source of ideas for ingredients that go well together.

SOURCES FOR IDEAS

One of the best sources for ideas about ingredients that go together is *The Flavor Bible: The Essential Guide to Culinary Creativity, Based on the Wisdom of America's Most Imaginative Chefs* by Karen Page and Andrew Dornenburg. Once you pick the first ingredient, you can then look for what combines with it. For example, you have cherries and find that they go well with red currants, or you have some figs and find they would go well with cilantro and lime. The book won't provide recipes or even ratios of the ingredients, but it should get you started on combinations to experiment with.

You can look at some of the juice combinations in your local grocery store for ideas on fruits that go together well. Taking a glance at modern cocktail recipes can also provide a starting point for interesting combinations; drinks that include so-called simple syrups will generally point to a medium-sweet or sweet mead. Cocktails that include sodas or sparkling water would indicate you could make a sparkling mead. Looking at desert recipes may give you some ideas on fruit and spice combinations generally as semisweet or sweet meads. The assortment of herbal teas commercially available can point to interesting blends to try in a metheglin. Looking at food recipes that emphasize unusual fruit or vegetable ingredients can suggest unusual mead recipes as well. Some of the unusual wine kits that use a combination of a varietal grape and fruit can even point to mead combinations. Braggots need grains, but there are many beer styles to consider as part of your recipe. One of the more unusual and tasty braggots was the

Moderation is the key when using spicy ingredients, especially because the age and quality of these ingredients may vary.

commercially brewed Mead the Gueuze, produced by Hanssens Artisanaal using their gueuze and lurgashall meads.

INITIAL QUANTITIES TO USE

The special ingredients can range from subtle to intense. You decide what level to target.

For moderate fruits, the quantities tend to range from 1–2 pounds (0.45–0.91 kilograms) of fruit per gallon (3.79 liters) of mead for a light fruit character to 4–5 (or more) pounds (1.81–2.27 kilograms) per gallon for a strong fruit character. Light fruits like plums and strawberries may need a lot more to achieve a significant fruit note in the mead. I've used as much as 25 pounds (11.34 kilograms) of strawberries in 6 gallons (22.7 liters) of mead, and the strawberry character was not really strong. For 5.5 gallons (20.82 liters) of pyment, I've used 3–4 gallons (11.36–15.14 liters) of grape juice for a strong grape (wine) character.

When using spices, moderation is the key. It is fairly easy to get too much spice character, and quantities are hard to predict since the age and quality of spices vary. Generally, 2–4 ounces (57–113 grams) is a lot in 5 gallons (19 liters) of mead. When you're starting to work with a new spice or spice blend, use significantly less than you think you will need and then use a tincture (see Chapter 8) to increase the spice level if necessary.

CHAPTER 10 RECIPES

EACH RECIPE IN THIS CHAPTER LISTS THE INGREDIENTS along with any special processing or treatment, as well as the yield, original gravity, and final gravity. Because the basic process for all mead recipes follows the steps described in Chapter 5, we won't repeat these steps here. Finings are not included in these recipes. Use them as necessary to finish your mead.

Any of the recipes can be scaled up or down in volume linearly. For example, to convert from 5 gallons (19 liters) to 6 gallons (22.7 liters), multiply all the ingredients by 1.2. To go from 5 gallons (19 liters) to 3.5 gallons (13.25 liters), multiply everything by 0.7. When scaling up, be sure to use more yeast; one packet of dry yeast per 3–7 gallons (11.4–26.5 liters) is OK, but try to stay in that range. When you scale down below 3 gallons (11.4 liters), you should use a scale to measure out the appropriate portion of a package of yeast.

Water quantities for each recipe are not included. Remember that water needs to be processed to eliminate the chlorine or chloramines. Either use a charcoal filter or treat the water with Campden tablets. (See Chapter 5.) You can adjust the specific gravity of the recipes by scaling back the fermentable ingredients or by adding more water. You may then back-sweeten or adjust the finish to get the final sweetness you desire.

STRAIGHT MEADS

Straight meads vary only in the varieties of honey used, the strength, and the finish, so you can easily change them around by using different honey varieties.

BUCKWHEAT

A straight buckwheat mead should appeal to those who love buckwheat pancakes. I developed this recipe with buckwheat honey purchased at the Minneapolis Farmers Market.
Makes 5 gallons (18.93 liters)

OG 1.080
FG 0.998

9.5 pounds (4.31 kilograms) buckwheat honey
0.18 ounce (5 grams) Go-Ferm
1 packet 71B-1122 yeast
0.14 ounce (4 grams) Fermaid K
0.28 ounce (8 grams) diammonium phosphate

ORANGE BLOSSOM

This recipe also appears in Chapter 5.
Makes 5 gallons (18.93 liters)

OG 1.115
FG 1.010

14 pounds (6.35 kilograms) orange blossom honey
0.18 ounce (5 grams) Go-Ferm
1 packet 71B-1122 yeast
0.14 ounce (4 grams) Fermaid K
0.28 ounce (8 grams) diammonium phosphate

TUPELO

This recipe is intended to finish medium-sweet to help bring out the tupelo characteristics.
Makes 5 gallons (18.93 liters)

OG 1.122
FG 1.017

14.5 pounds (6.58 kilograms) tupelo honey
0.18 ounce (5 grams) Go-Ferm
1 packet 71B-1122 yeast
0.14 ounce (4 grams) Fermaid K
0.28 ounce (8 grams) diammonium phosphate

PYMENTS

The pyment recipes below were developed with fresh wine grape juice that typically has a specific gravity in the 1.090–1.100 range. You could also start with the juice from a high-quality wine kit, add the honey, stir to dissolve, and then add treated water to get to the target original gravity. While you can also create a pyment by mixing a straight mead and a homemade wine post-fermentation, the recipes below are based on the grape juice being added during the primary fermentation.

CHARDONNAY

The fruity, floral, herbal, and sometimes woody character of tupelo honey goes well with Chardonnay, since many Americans are used to oak-aged wines. This pyment can also stand up to additional oak treatment.

Chardonnay is a wine variety that benefits from aging *sur lie*, or "on the lees." Once I transfer the mead from the plastic primary to glass, I leave it sitting on the yeast (lees) for approximately two months beyond when the fermentation appears to have stopped. The sur lie process can add creaminess and a bready, toasty character to the mead, can reduce the fruit character, and can add a yeasty taste. If you want to try the sur lie process, taste your mead every week or so and rack off the lees when you think you have the flavors at the level you prefer. Temperature influences the speed of the process; cellar temperature (55°F or 13°C) is traditional.

Makes 5.5 gallons (20.82 liters)

OG 1.120

FG 1.026

9.25 pounds (4.2 kilograms) tupelo honey

3 gallons (11.35 liters) Chardonnay juice

1 vial White Labs WLP730 Chardonnay yeast

2 quarts (1.89 liter) apple juice for yeast starter

0.14 ounce (4 grams) Fermaid K

0.28 ounce (8 grams) diammonium phosphate

GEWÜRZTRAMINER

This recipe uses tupelo honey, but you can make this pyment with most light-flavored honeys, such as clover or orange blossom.

Makes 5 gallons (18.93 liters)

OG 1.118

FG 1.010

8.67 pounds (3.94 kilograms) tupelo honey

2.5 gallons (9.46 liters) Gewürztraminer juice

1 packet 71B-1122 yeast

0.18 ounce (5 grams) Go-Ferm

0.14 ounce (4 grams) Fermaid K

0.28 ounce (8 grams) diammonium phosphate

MUSCAT

Muscat grapes have been cultivated for winemaking for centuries. California growers have several different varieties of muscat under cultivation—all slightly different but still distinctly muscat. Even when fermented to dryness (final gravity below 1.000), the wines still have a slight sweetness. To take advantage of that subliminal sweetness, this pyment targets a drier finish than the earlier pyment recipes.

Makes 5 gallons (18.93 liters)

OG 1.110

FG 1.002

8.76 pounds (3.98 kilograms) orange blossom honey

2 gallons (7.57 liters) muscat juice

1 packet 71B-1122 yeast

0.18 ounce (5 grams) Go-Ferm

0.14 ounce (4 grams) Fermaid K

0.28 ounce (8 grams) diammonium phosphate

SANGIOVESE

Sangiovese grapes are frequently used in the production of wines like Chianti and Carmignano; they are blended into many domestic red wines; and they can be processed in a single varietal wine. The grapes are fairly high in acidity, with strong notes of fruits (cherry, strawberry, and plum) and spices like black pepper, as well as notes of tobacco leaves. The high acidity works well in pyment production because the acid and the tannins help balance the residual sweetness.

Makes 5 gallons (18.93 liters)

> OG 1.122
>
> FG 1.015

> 8.93 pounds (4.05 kilograms) wildflower honey
>
> 2.58 gallons (9.78 liters) Sangiovese juice
>
> 1 packet 71B-1122 yeast
>
> 0.18 ounce (5 grams) Go-Ferm
>
> 0.14 ounce (4 grams) Fermaid K
>
> 0.28 ounce (8 grams) diammonium phosphate

CYSERS

APPLE

The key to a good cyser is the apple juice. Traditional cider apples are not available in most of the United States, and most commercial apple juice is blended to be consumed unfermented. Try sourcing apple juice that makes a good hard cider and remember that the specific gravity of the juice will vary with the variety of apples used. You can also substitute pear juice for most or all of the apple juice to make a pear-based cyser.

Makes 5 gallons (18.93 liters)

> OG 1.122
>
> FG 1.015

> 10.5 pounds (4.76 kilograms) clover honey
>
> 4 gallons (15.16 liters) apple juice
>
> 1 packet 71B-1122 yeast
>
> 0.18 ounce (5 grams) Go-Ferm
>
> 0.14 ounce (4 grams) Fermaid K
>
> 0.28 ounce (8 grams) diammonium phosphate

FRUIT MEAD
BERRY MEAD

BLACK CURRANT

Black currants, while pungent, acidic, and slightly earthy, make fantastic meads. The crème de cassis liqueur is based on black currants, but most Americans are unfamiliar with the berries. The amount of fruit required for this recipe will contribute about 2.5 gallons (9.5 liters) of water to the mead, so the original gravity listed is from before the fruit addition. The effective original gravity after the fruit addition will be about 1.126. The volume before the fruit will be approximately 3.6 gallons (13.6 liters).

Sanitize a large mesh bag by boiling it in water for a few minutes, and then fill it with berries before tying it shut. When you're ready to rack the mead to a carboy, save the bag of currants for use in another mead; there isn't much fermentable left in the berries, but they can still impart a lot flavor to the next mead. (Try them in the pomegranate–black currant mead below.) I do wring the bag of berries a little to extract some of the finished mead, but don't aggressively press the berries if they are going into another batch of mead. Makes 6 gallons (22.71 liters)

> OG 1.192 (before fruit addition—effective OG 1.125)
>
> FG 1.010
>
>
> 16.5 pounds (7.49 kilograms) wildflower honey
>
> 24.25 pounds (11.01 kilograms) black currants
>
> 1 packet 71B-1122 yeast
>
> 0.18 ounce (5 grams) Go-Ferm
>
> 0.14 ounce (4 grams) Fermaid K
>
> 0.28 ounce (8 grams) diammonium phosphate

BLACK RASPBERRY

Black raspberries have a softer, less acidic character than red raspberries, but they're much more intense, so you'll need much less fruit than in a red raspberry melomel. The volume before the fruit addition is 4.4 gallons (16.7 liters), and the fruit will add about 0.6 gallons (2.3 liters) of water to the mead. The target final gravity is medium-sweet to emphasize the fruit.

Makes 5 gallons (18.93 liters; final volume)

> OG 1.137 (before fruit addition; effective OG 1.123)
>
> FG 1.015
>
>
> 14.3 pounds (6.49 kilograms) orange blossom honey
>
> 5.94 pounds (2.7 kilograms) black raspberries
>
> 1 packet 71B-1122 yeast
>
> 0.18 ounce (5 grams) Go-Ferm
>
> 0.14 ounce (4 grams) Fermaid K
>
> 0.28 ounce (8 grams) diammonium phosphate

CHOKEBERRY

See Chapter 3 for details on processing chokeberries into juice. The blend of honey isn't important, because the chokeberries have an intense flavor that will overwhelm most honeys. The mead will be intentionally quite sweet to offset some of the high concentration of tannins in the fruit. The dark burgundy or purple mead is intense, and with all the antioxidants in the fruit, the mead has the potential to age well. Mead made with chokeberries is unusual. People who like chokeberry or chokecherry jelly love it, and those who don't like the jelly don't like the mead. It is, however, a good mead to use for blending when you want to add tannins or structure to another mead.

Add the honey to the juice—the berries produce just over 1 gallon (3.79 liters) of juice—and stir to dissolve. Then add treated water to hit the target original gravity.

Makes 5 gallons (18.93 liters)

> OG 1.142
>
> FG 1.036

> 6 pounds (2.72 kilograms) saw palmetto honey
>
> 3 pounds (1.36 kilograms) wildflower honey
>
> 9 pounds (4.09 kilograms) orange blossom honey
>
> 8.75 pounds (3.75 kilograms) chokeberries processed into juice
>
> 1 packet 71B-1122 yeast
>
> 0.18 ounce (5 grams) Go-Ferm
>
> 0.14 ounce (4 grams) Fermaid K
>
> 0.28 ounce (8 grams) diammonium phosphate

ELDERBERRY

See Chapter 3 for details on processing elderberries. The elderberry juice I used to develop this recipe had an specific gravity of 1.050, but it can vary a little from year to year. This mead will be a dark burgundy color and will have an indistinct fruity character with earthy undertones. (Most people are not familiar with the berry and don't recognize the flavor.) A few home wine recipes also call for dried elderberries for the fruit character they add.

Start by adding the honey to the juice and stir to dissolve. Then add treated water to hit the target original gravity.

Makes 5 gallons (18.93 liters)

> OG 1.122
>
> FG 1.012

> 13.5 pounds (6.13 kilograms) orange blossom honey
>
> 0.875 gallons (3.32 liters) elderberry juice
>
> 1 packet D-47 yeast
>
> 0.18 ounce (5 grams) Go-Ferm
>
> 0.14 ounce (4 grams) Fermaid K
>
> 0.28 ounce (8 grams) diammonium phosphate

MIXED BERRY

This is a big, strong, sweet, and berry-oriented melomel. Various blends of fruit are available in large bags in the freezer sections of grocery stores and big-box discount stores, but the ratio of fruits and even the types of fruit will vary. The volume before the fruit is 3.16 gallons (11.96 liters), and the fruit will add about 1.84 gallons (6.97 liters) of water to the mead. I put the fruit in a large sanitized mesh bag.

Makes 5 gallons (18.93 liters; final volume)

OG 1.206 (before fruit addition; effective OG about 1.138)

FG 1.032

15.5 pounds (7.04 kilograms) clover blossom honey

18 pounds (8.17 kilograms) frozen berry mix (raspberries, blueberries, blackberries)

1 packet 71B-1122 yeast

0.18 ounce (5 grams) Go-Ferm

0.14 ounce (4 grams) Fermaid K

0.28 ounce (8 grams) diammonium phosphate

POMEGRANATE

This one is a tad over the BJCP limit for a hydromel. The pomegranate juice I used to develop this recipe had an specific gravity of 1.072. Add the honey to the juice and stir to dissolve, then add treated water to hit the original gravity.

Makes 5 gallons (18.93 liters)

OG 1.085

FG 1.001

7 pounds (3.18 kilograms) orange blossom honey

1.875 gallons (7.1 liters) pomegranate juice

1 packet 71B-1122 yeast

0.18 ounce (5 grams) Go-Ferm

0.14 ounce (4 grams) Fermaid K

0.28 ounce (8 grams) diammonium phosphate

POMEGRANATE–BLACK CURRANT

The black currants in this recipe come from the previous black currant batch (see the black currant recipe on page 128), so they won't be adding much if any fermentable sugar to the mead, but they will contribute some black currant aroma and flavor.

Makes 5 gallons (18.93 liters)

OG 1.140 (before adding bag of black currants to fermenter)

FG 1.025

13.25 pounds (6.22 kilograms) orange blossom honey

2 gallons (7.58 liters) pomegranate juice

24.5 pounds (11.12 kilograms) black currants (from previous batch)

1 packet 71B-1122 yeast

0.18 ounce (5 grams) Go-Ferm

0.14 ounce (4 grams) Fermaid K

0.28 ounce (8 grams) diammonium phosphate

RASPBERRY

The raspberry is an 8:1 concentrate in this recipe; 1 quart (0.9 liter) equals 2 gallons (7.6 liters) of juice. The target is a medium-sweet finish to provide some support for the raspberries. Pour the concentrate and honey into the fermenter and then start adding water.

Makes 5 gallons (18.93 liters)

   OG 1.120

   FG 1.013

14 pounds (6.35 kilograms) orange blossom honey

1 quart (0.95 liters) raspberry concentrate

1 packet 71B-1122 yeast

0.18 ounce (5 grams) Go-Ferm

0.14 ounce (4 grams) Fermaid K

0.28 ounce (8 grams) diammonium phosphate

MELOMEL

BLACKBERRY–CHARDONNAY

The ingredients for this mead combine some of those traditionally used in a melomel and some in a pyment, so it is categorized as a BJCP melomel. The volume before fruit will be 4.63 gallons (17.5 liters), and the blackberries will add about 0.37 gallons (1.4 liters) of water.

Makes 5 gallons (18.93 liters; final volume)

   OG 1.136 (before fruit addition)

   FG 1.018

11.75 pounds (5.33 kilograms) orange blossom honey

1.5 gallons (5.7 liters) Chardonnay grape juice

3.625 pounds (1.65 kilograms) blackberries

1 packet 71B-1122 yeast

0.18 ounce (5 grams) Go-Ferm

0.14 ounce (4 grams) Fermaid K

0.28 ounce (8 grams) diammonium phosphate

POMEGRANATE–BLACK CURRANT–TART CHERRY

The volume before the berries will be approximately 4.15 gallons (15.73 liters), and the whole fruit will add approximately 0.85 gallons (3.22 liters) of water to the mead. Add the honey to the fruit juices and stir to dissolve, then add treated water to hit the target original gravity. I place the berries in a sanitized mesh bag and place the bag in the primary.

Makes 5 gallons (18.93 liters; final volume)

OG 1.143 (before adding berries)

FG 1.012

10.5 pounds (4.76 kilograms) wildflower honey

1.5 gallons (5.69 liters) pomegranate juice

0.5 gallons (1.9 liters) tart cherry juice

8.6 pounds (3.9 kilograms) black currants

1 packet 71B-1122 yeast

0.18 ounce (5 grams) Go-Ferm

0.14 ounce (4 grams) Fermaid K

0.28 ounce (8 grams) diammonium phosphate

SANGIOVESE–ZINFANDEL–BLACK CURRANT

This recipe includes ingredients from both a melomel and a pyment, so it is categorized as a BJCP melomel. The volume before fruit will be 4 gallons (15.16 liters), and the currants will add about 1 gallon (3.79 liters) of water.

Makes 5 gallons (18.93 liters; final volume)

OG 1.174 (before fruit addition; effective OG 1.139)

FG 1.020 (I got better than expected attenuation)

14 pounds (6.36 kilograms) orange blossom honey

0.5 gallon (1.9 liters) Zinfandel grape juice

0.667 gallon (2.53 liters) Sangiovese grape juice

9.5 pounds (4.31 kilograms) black currants

1 packet 71B-1122 yeast

0.18 ounce (5 grams) Go-Ferm

0.14 ounce (4 grams) Fermaid K

0.28 ounce (8 grams) diammonium phosphate

STONE FRUIT MEAD

PEACH MANGO

The volume before the fruit is approximately 3.75 gallons (14.2 liters), and the fruit will add approximately 5 quarts (4.74 liters) of water.

Makes 5 gallons (18.93 liters; final volume)

OG 1.162 (before fruit addition)

FG 1.017

7 pounds (3.18 kilograms) peaches, peeled and pitted

5 pounds (2.27 kilograms) mangoes, peeled and pitted

14.5 pounds (6.58 kilograms) wildflower honey

1 packet 71B-1122 yeast

0.18 ounce (5 grams) Go-Ferm

0.14 ounce (4 grams) Fermaid K

0.28 ounce (8 grams) diammonium phosphate

SPICED MEAD
FRUIT AND SPICE MEAD

RASPBERRY–HOT PEPPER

This recipe is a variation of the mesquite-chipotle metheglin on p.134. Including different varieties of dried pepper increases the complexity of the mead; I like a combination of chipotle, ancho (dried poblano), and guajillo. Keep the raspberry level low to let the other characteristics show. The volume before the fruit is approximately 4.7 gallons (1.78 liters), and the fruit will add about 0.3 gallons (1.14 liters) of water.

Makes 5 gallons (18.93 liters; final volume)

OG 1.128 (before fruit)

FG 1.014

14.25 pounds (6.47 kilograms) mesquite blossom honey

3 pounds (1.36 kilograms) raspberries

2 dried peppers

4 dried peppers (for tincture)

1 cup (0.24 liter) vodka (for tincture)

1 packet 71B-1122 yeast

0.18 ounce (5 grams) Go-Ferm

0.14 ounce (4 grams) Fermaid K

0.28 ounce (8 grams) diammonium phosphate

STRAWBERRY–BANANA–GINGER

The batch size before the fruit addition is approximately 2.5 gallons (9.46 liters), and the strawberries will add approximately 2.5 gallons (9.46 liters) of water and just over 1 pound (0.45 kilograms) of fermentable sugar to the mead. Your hydrometer or refractometer probably won't be able to read as high as 1.254. The easy way to measure this mead is to dilute the must; mix equal volumes of the must and water and then measure the specific gravity. The diluted must should read 1.127. Add the bananas once the mead is transferred to a carboy; just peel the bananas and force them through the carboy neck.

Makes 5 gallons (18.93 liters; final volume)

  OG 1.254 (before adding fruit; effective OG approximately 1.137)

  FG is 1.020

  15 pounds (6.81 kilograms) wildflower honey

  23 pounds (10.43 kilograms) strawberries

  0.5 pound (0.23 kilograms) ginger (thin slices)

  4 bananas (very ripe)

  1 packet 71B-1122 yeast

  0.18 ounce (5 grams) Go-Ferm

  0.14 ounce (4 grams) Fermaid K

  0.28 ounce (8 grams) diammonium phosphate

SPICE, HERB, OR VEGETABLE MEAD

MESQUITE–CHIPOTLE

Mesquite honey just seems to cry out for smoky chipotles. I like a little of the heat from the peppers, but I also want to be able to taste the honey, so to avoid getting too much chipotle character, I just put 2 whole chipotles into the mead when I transfer it to a carboy. At that time I also place 4 chipotles in a pint jar and cover them with vodka; screw the lid on and let the tincture develop while the mead finishes fermentation. When you are ready to package the mead, you can adjust the chipotle character with some of the tincture.

Makes 5 gallons (18.93 liters)

  OG 1.120

  FG 1.014

  14.25 pounds (6.47 kilograms) mesquite blossom honey

  2 chipotles

  4 chipotles (for tincture)

  1 cup (0.24 liter) vodka (for tincture)

  1 packet 71B-1122 yeast

  0.18 ounce (5 grams) Go-Ferm

  0.14 ounce (4 grams) Fermaid K

  0.28 ounce (8 grams) diammonium phosphate

NOT MARY ANNE–GINGER

An adult beverage form of ginger ale, this mead is very ginger-forward. Place the ginger slices in a sanitized mesh bag in the primary. When finished, stabilize and sweeten the mead to balance the ginger and force-carbonate to around 3.0 volumes of carbon dioxide. The carbonation will balance some of the residual sweetness.

Makes 5 gallons (18.93 liters)

OG 1.140

FG 1.030

16.67 pounds (7.57 kilograms) raspberry blossom honey

3.125 pounds (1.42 kilograms) ginger (thin slices)

1 packet 71B-1122 yeast

0.18 ounces (5 grams) Go-Ferm

0.14 ounce (4 grams) Fermaid K

0.28 ounce (8 grams) diammonium phosphate

SPEARMINT

This mead uses dried commercial spearmint leaves that dominate, but the fairly high sweetness does help with the perception of the mint. The mead blends nicely with the bourbon barrel mead on p.138. The initial ¾ pound of spearmint should be sanitized with just enough vodka to dampen the leaves and then placed in a sanitized mesh bag and added to the primary fermenter. At the same time, prepare the tincture by placing another ¼ pound of leaves in a large jar and covering them with vodka. When the mead is ready for packaging, use the tincture to adjust the mint level to taste. If you have the equipment, force-carbonate to approximately 3.0 volumes of carbon dioxide.

Makes 5 gallons (18.93 liters)

OG 1.140

FG 1.030

16.67 pounds (7.25 kilograms) wildflower honey

0.75 pounds (0.34 kilograms) dried spearmint

0.25 pounds (0.11 kilograms) dried spearmint (for tincture)

0.18 ounce (5 grams) Go-Ferm

0.14 ounce (4 grams) Fermaid K

0.28 ounce (8 grams) diammonium phosphate

SPECIALTY MEAD
BRAGGOTS

There are two approaches to creating a braggot. The first introduces the honey and the beer wort in the primary fermentation. The second involves a post-fermentation blend of a mead and a homemade beer.

DRY-HOPPED BRAGGOT

You create this braggot by fermenting beer wort that has had an additional braggot honey dose added after the wort has been chilled to fermentation temperature. Do not boil the honey.

BRAGGOT

Makes 6 gallons (22.71 liters)

> OG 1.118
>
> FG 1.010

The beer portion of the recipe uses an all-grain approach and assumes a system efficiency of 70 percent; add the honey to the fermenter first, and then run in the chilled wort. Mash the malt at 150°F (66°C) with 1.33 quarts (1.26 liters) of water per 1 pound (0.5 kilogram) of malt. This part of the recipe requires the following ingredients:

- 9.45 pounds (4.29 kilograms) pilsner malt
- 1.18 pounds (0.54 kilogram) dark Munich malt
- 0.95 pound (0.43 kilogram) Crystal 40L malt
- 0.47 pound (0.21 kilogram) Victory malt
- 0.82 ounce (23 grams) Crystal hops (60 minutes)
- 1.38 ounces (39 grams) Crystal hops (15 minutes)
- 1.38 ounces (39 grams) Crystal hops (1 minute)
- 1.0 ounce (28 grams) Crystal hops (dry hop)

The mead portion of the recipe includes just the staggered nutrients and the yeast. Adjust the honey quantity to hit the target original gravity. Once the braggot has finished fermenting, it is time to add the dry hops. Leave the mead on the dry hops 7–10 days, and then package the mead. Most people expect beer to be carbonated, so to help emphasize the beer aspect of the braggot, carbonate it to a beer level. The recipe requires the following additional ingredients:

8.5 pounds (3.86 kilograms) wildflower honey

1 packet 71B-1122 yeast

0.18 ounce (5 grams) Go-Ferm

0.14 ounce (4 grams) Fermaid K

0.28 ounce (8 grams) diammonium phosphate

SMOKED BRAGGOT

This braggot is created by blending beer and mead post-fermentation.

WORT

Makes 5.5 gallons (20.82 liters)

OG 1.056

FG 1.012

The beer portion of the recipe uses an all-grain approach and assumes a system efficiency of 70 percent. Mash the malt in a step process with rests at 149°F (65°C) and 158°F (70°C) using 1.33 quarts (1.26 liters) of water per 1 pound (0.45 kilogram) of malt. The liquid yeast should be processed in a 2-liter starter on a stir plate, starting a day before the beer is brewed. The recipe requires the following ingredients:

11.28 pounds (5.12 kilograms) Rauchmalt (German smoked malt)

0.25 pound (0.11 kilogram) Carafa III dehusked malt

0.29 pound (0.13 kilogram) Vienna malt

1 ounce (28 grams) Hallertauer hops (60 minutes)

0.5 ounce (14 grams) Hallertauer hops (10 minutes)

1 vial White Labs WLP830 German lager yeast

The mead used for blending during recipe development was a medium-sweet straight mead made with wildflower honey that had an final gravity of 1.018 and an original gravity of 1.125. For this particular combination, the selected blend was 6 parts of mead to 4 parts of beer. Remember, depending on your mead and your beer, your blending ratio may be significantly different. See the blending section of Chapter 8.

EXPERIMENTAL MEAD

BOURBON BARREL

The hydromel in this recipe should be fermented out and then aged in a used 8-gallon bourbon barrel for 3 weeks. The barrel's bourbon character will push the alcohol level beyond the typical hydromel range. The batch size will be slightly over the barrel volume, so that the barrel will be full with a little left to top up. When aging your mead in a bourbon barrel, you need to evaluate it every few days to see how the bourbon and wood characteristics are changing. Once you hit the levels you like, you need to transfer the mead out of the barrel into a carboy or keg.

The mead finishes very dry and because of the alcohol from the barrel, it seems even drier than the hydrometer shows. When combined with some mint simple syrup and garnished with a mint leaf, it makes a tasty mint julep. An interesting option might be to stabilize and then back-sweeten this mead with a mint syrup (made from honey and mint leaves) to the level of a mint julep and then to carbonate it to the level of a cocktail.
Makes 9 gallons (34.07 liters)

OG 1.080

FG 0.995

17 pounds (7.72 kilograms) mesquite honey

2 packets 71B-1122 yeast

0.36 ounce (10 grams) Go-Ferm

0.28 ounce (8 grams) Fermaid K

0.56 ounce (16 grams) diammonium phosphate

MESQUITE–AGAVE

Agave nectar is a sweetener derived from the agave plant. It is usually available in three grades or colors: light, amber, and dark. The light version has little flavor beyond the sweetness; the amber shows some caramel-like characteristics; and the dark version has even more caramel-like notes. I find the amber or dark version work best for meads. The agave nectar has roughly the same effect on the original gravity as the equivalent weight of honey. Use of agave nectar in this essentially straight mead puts it in the BJCP's Experimental Mead category. You could also ferment the mead and the agave nectar separately and then blend for taste post-fermentation.
Makes 5 gallons (18.93 liters)

OG 1.120

FG 1.014

8.25 pounds (3.75 kilograms) mesquite blossom honey

6 pounds (2.72 kilograms) amber agave nectar

1 packet 71B-1122 yeast

0.18 ounce (5 grams) Go-Ferm

0.14 ounce (4 grams) Fermaid K

0.28 ounce (8 grams) diammonium phosphate

SLUDGE MEAD

Sludge mead, which isn't really based on a recipe, came from my friend Curt Stock's idea to save all that sludge (sediment and very cloudy mead) from the bottom of the carboy and combine it with other sludge to eventually extract some mead from it as it settles. Obviously, using the sludge from an infected mead is not a good idea. Likewise, some meads (particularly metheglins) may not meld well with other meads. Generally, melomels combine well with each other, and most pyments will combine with each other. Combining the meads may result in a renewed fermentation, depending on what you are combining. Finishing a sludge mead for balance should be handled just as for any other mead.

In one case, I combined the sludge from three different white wine grape pyments—a tupelo Chardonnay, a tupelo Gewürztraminer, and a mixed white wine—into a small carboy as I packaged the meads. The resultant mead was kegged once most of the sediment became a compact layer on the bottom. I didn't get a lot of mead—probably less than 1.5 gallons (5.7 liters)—but it was essentially a free byproduct of the other three meads.

Other interesting sludge meads have resulted from the sludge of batches of black currant, raspberry, cherry, and other berry meads. Sludge from red wine grape pyments will combine nicely with the sludge from many berry melomels. A mead salvaged from the sludge of traditional meads made with varietal honeys is worth trying, though it probably is a good idea to leave the buckwheat sludge out of the combination.

CHAPTER

II | TROUBLESHOOTING

TROUBLESHOOTING REQUIRES IDENTIFYING A FLAW CORRECTLY so you can apply the proper solution to the problem. A book by itself cannot help you identify all the flaws, because that may require some sensory training—learning the aroma or taste of various flaws. A homebrew club can be a great place for sensory training with fellow meadmakers. Some flaws in mead are similar to those in beer, while others are more like the flaws in wine.

Braggot, as both a mead and a beer, can exhibit faults from both, but the beer-specific faults are not covered here.

FAULTS

If your mead exhibits a characteristic in the first column, look at the descriptions in the second column, then read on to learn about causes and controls for the fault. Items in the second column in **bold** have a longer description on page 143.

Characteristic	Fault
Acetic	**Acetic acid**
Acetone	Ethyl acetate, higher alcohols, poor sanitation, hot fermentation, insufficient yeast, insufficient nutrients
Acidic	Contamination from poor sanitation, too much acid added, underripe fruit
Almond	**Oxidation**
Band-aid	**Phenolic**
Barnyard	Contamination from *Brettanomyces*
Bitter flavor	**Sulfur dioxide, oxidation**
Black tea–like	**Astringent**
Browning color	**Oxidation**
Burnt matches	**Sulfur dioxide**
Burnt rubber	**Mercaptans, disulfides**
Butter, butterscotch	**Diacetyl**
Cabbage	**Disulfides**
Canned vegetables	**Disulfides**
Celery	**Sorbate**
Cloudy	**Haze, oxidation**
Clove	**Phenolic**
Cloying	See *flabby*
Cooked cabbage	**Mercaptans, disulfides**
Dried straw or hay	**Acetaldehyde**
Electrical fire	**Phenolic**
Fermentation doesn't finish	**Stuck ferment**
Flabby	Excessive, unbalanced sweetness
Fruity	Fermented too warm, yeast choice, low nutrients, high OG, honey variety
Fusel alcohols	Fermented too warm, insufficient yeast, insufficient nutrients
Garlic, spoiled	**Hydrogen sulfide**
Geranium; aroma of crushed geranium leaves	**Geranium**
Green apple	**Acetaldehyde**
Hay or dried straw	**Acetaldehyde**
Hazelnut	**Oxidation**
Hot	Fermented too warm, insufficient yeast, insufficient nutrients
Juicy Fruit gum	**Sorbate**
Medicinal	**Phenolic**

Characteristic	Fault
Metallic	**Acetaldehyde, sulfur dioxide,** rusted equipment, water, too much nutrient
Metallic flavor	**Sulfur dioxide**
Mousy	Contamination from *Brettanomyces*, lactic acid bacteria
Movie theater popcorn, rancid butter	**Diacetyl**
Musty, stale dishcloth, swampy	**Malolactic fermentation**
Nail polish remover	Ethyl acetate, higher alcohols, poor sanitation, hot fermentation, insufficient yeast, insufficient nutrients
Nutty	**Oxidation**
Onion	**Disulfides**
Papery	**Oxidation**
Pineapple	**Sorbate**
Plastic	**Phenolic**
Rancid	**Sorbate**
Rancid butter	**Diacetyl**
Roasted nuts	**Acetaldehyde**
Rotten eggs	**Hydrogen sulfide**
Rubbery	**Disulfides**
Sauerkraut	Lactic acid, poor sanitation
Sewer gas	**Hydrogen sulfide**
Sherry	**Acetaldehyde, oxidation**
Skunk	**Mercaptans**
Soapy	Residual cleaners and **disulphides**
Solvent	Ethyl acetate, higher alcohols: fermented too warm, insufficient yeast, insufficient nutrients
Sour	**Acetaldehyde**
Sourness	Excess acids, see *acidic*
Spoiled garlic	**Hydrogen sulfide**
Stale	**Oxidation**
Strong sulfur aroma	**Sulfur dioxide**
Sweaty	Contamination from *Brettanomyces*, lactic acid bacteria
Sweet	**Stuck ferment**: incomplete fermentation, OG too high, too much back sweetening
Tannic	**Astringent**
Tart	See *acidic*
Tea	**Astringent**
Unexpected bottle fermentation or carbonation	Poor sanitation, bottled before fermentation finished
Vegetal	**Disulfides,** poor sanitation, long lag time
Vinegar	Ethyl acetate, **acetic acid**
Walnut	**Oxidation**
Warming	High ethanol content
Wet cardboard	**Oxidation**
Yogurt	Lactic acid, poor sanitation

by adding sulfur dioxide to the mead. At high levels of oxidation, the mead may begin to show sherry characteristics and become nutty. Adding a small amount of sulfites (metabisulfite HSO_3) as prophylactic antioxidants can also be a good idea.

PHENOLIC

Causes of phenols include wild yeast contamination due to poor sanitation or chlorine or chloramines present in the water. Control with proper sanitation during the entire production process. Always process water to remove chlorine or chloramines.

SORBATE

Potassium sorbate additions result in sorbic acid in the mead, which some people perceive as a rancid character. The sorbic acid breaks down into ethyl sorbate over time, which has notes of candied or artificial fruit, Juicy Fruit gum, celery, and pineapple. The time it takes for sorbate to become ethyl sorbate depends on temperature, pH level, alcohol level, and other factors, but the transformation will typically happen in 6–12 months.

STUCK FERMENT

Temperature variations can cause stuck fermentation due to the impacts of the increasing alcohol on the yeast membranes. Symptoms include a higher-than-expected specific gravity—higher than the yeast's alcohol tolerance indicates it should be. You can prevent stuck fermentations best by using enough yeast, hydrating the yeast properly, maintaining a constant and proper fermentation temperature, providing the nutrients at the proper intervals, and stirring at the proper times.

Recovery requires restarting fermentation, so make sure it really is stuck and isn't just at the yeast's alcohol limit. First try to get the mead into the 70–75°F (21–24 °C) range to see if that will get the yeast back to work. If that doesn't work, the process gets more complicated. The idea is to start a new batch of yeast working with a small amount of the stuck mead and then to double the volume of the restarted batch every time fermentation restarts. You need to rehydrate (or grow a new starter) of the yeast, put about 0.25 gallons (0.9 liter) of the stuck mead into a sanitized carboy, and add the new yeast to it. It should show signs of renewed fermentation within a day. Once it is fermenting, add another 0.25 gallon (0.9 liter) of the stuck mead, wait for it to start fermenting, and then add 0.5 more gallons (1.9 liters) of the stuck mead. Once that shows signs of fermenting, add 1 gallon (3.79 liters) of the stuck mead. Continue doubling the volume (until you have added all the stuck mead) each time it shows signs of fermentation.

SULFUR DIOXIDE

Typically a result of excessive sulfite (SO_2) or metabisulfite (HSO_3) additions. Overuse of sulfur dioxide can leave a mead with matchstick, burnt rubber, mothball, metallic, or bitter characteristics. If too much is added initially, it can keep fermentation from even starting, but some can be removed by aerating the mead. Some sulfites occur naturally in the mead, and at proper levels, sulfites serve as antimicrobial agents, antioxidants, or antibrowning agents. In the wine world, the optimal level is considered to be around 100 ppm—more can be perceived as a flaw and lower is insufficient to protect the wine—but the form of the sulfite (bound or unbound) matters. In general, I do not add sulfites to my finished meads.

GLOSSARY

ABV – Alcohol by Volume. The measurement of the alcohol content in mead expressed as a percentage of the total volume.

AHA – American Homebrewers Association. An organization of home beer-, mead-, and cidermakers. See www.homebrewersassociation.org.

alcohol limit – For yeast, the alcohol level sufficient to stop the fermentation process. A yeast strain's stated alcohol limit can sometimes be exceeded, but it usually takes a lot of extra effort to get the yeast to continue fermenting in the presence of high alcohol levels.

atemperation – The process of slowly adjusting the yeast culture to the temperature of the must. See Chapter 9.

attenuation – The degree of conversion of sugar to alcohol and CO_2 through fermentation. Or, put another way, the percentage of the sugar that the yeast consumed. Computed as:

$$\frac{(OG - FG)}{(OG - 1.0)} \times 100$$

balance – In mead, the complex synergy of aroma, flavor, structure, sweetness, and mouthfeel. Balance in mead differs from balance in beer, which is simply the proportion of malt flavor and sweetness to hop flavor and bitterness. See Chapter 6.

BJCP – Beer Judge Certification Program. The organization that writes the style descriptions used to judge competitions for homemade beer, mead, and cider. The BJCP also certifies judges. See www.bjcp.org.

braggot – A mead that includes grains, typically malted barley.

carbonation – The fizz added to beverages by dissolved carbon dioxide (CO_2). The BJCP has three levels of carbonation, in increasing order: still, petillant, and sparkling.

cloying – A sweet character that is not balanced by acidity or tannins.

cyser – A melomel in which the fruit used is apples, either fresh or as juice.

DAP – Diammonium phosphate, $(NH_2)_2HPO_4$. A yeast nutrient used mainly to provide free nitrogen to the yeast.

dry yeast – See *yeast*.

ethanol – The dominant alcohol produced by fermentation and the intoxicating agent in alcoholic beverages. Ethanol is the oldest recreational drug still used by mankind.

fermentation – A complex biological process whereby yeast converts mead must into mead. At a high level, the yeast converts the simple sugars into alcohol and carbon dioxide. However, many lesser reactions contribute to the complex aromas and flavors of the mead.

final gravity (FG) – A measurement of the remaining sugar content of mead following fermentation that is based on the density of the fluid.

finings – Adjuncts added to mead to improve the clarity of the final product.

flabby – A mead generally lacking in structure, usually acidity, specifically.

flat – Describes a mead with no effervescence. Also referred to as a *still mead*. See *carbonation*.

flocculation – The process of yeast cells clumping together and then settling to the bottom of the fermenter.

fusels – A mixture of several alcohols, but mainly amyl alcohol, resulting from fermentation. Fusels can be perceived as spicy, hot, or solvent-like. They are the result of higher fermentation temperature, lower pH fermentation, and limited nutrient fermentation. Also known as *fusel alcohols* and *fusel oils*.

hydromel – The lowest strength meads, typically with an original gravity of 1.035–1.080 and 3.5–7.5% ABV.

hydrometer – An instrument used to measure specific gravity. Typically, hydrometers are made from glass. Many common versions sold in homebrew supply stores are the so-called triple-scale style with scales for specific gravity, specific gravity as degrees Plato, and potential alcohol that will result if the mead is fermented to a specific gravity of 1.000.

liquid yeast – See *yeast*.

melomel – A mead made with the addition of fruit.

metheglin – A mead made with the addition of spices.

mouthfeel – A description of how mead feels in the mouth. Includes considerations such as body, texture, alcoholic warmth, and carbonation.

must – Mead before it is fermented. Derived from wine-making terminology.

original gravity (OG) – A measurement of the sugar content of must prior to fermentation based on the density of the fluid.

oxidation – A common flaw in meads that can result in changes in color, flavor, and aroma. Oxidation can occur throughout the mead-making process, even after packaging. Oxidation can occur without oxygen actually being present; it simply means that a chemical compound in the mead has lost electrons while another compound has gained them.

pectin – A gelling agent common in most fruits. It can cause a haze in meads that is difficult to remove.

pectinase – An enzyme (also known as pectin enzyme) that will break down the pectin in a fruit so that it does not form a haze.

pettilant – Describes a moderately sparkling mead between *still* and *sparkling*. See *carbonation*.

pH – A measurement of the acidity or alkalinity of an aqueous solution on a scale of 1 to 14. A value of 7 represents a neutral solution (pure water has a pH of nearly 7). Values less than 7 represent acidic solutions and those greater than 7 are alkaline.

ppm – Parts per million.

pyment – A melomel in which the fruits used are grapes, either fresh or as juice.

refractometer – An optical instrument used to determine the sugar content of a solution. The instrument works by measuring the light refraction of the solution. Though some report in degrees Plato or even in specific gravity, classic refractometers report specific gravity in degrees Brix (1 degree Brix represents 1% by weight as sucrose). A conversion table or calculator must be used to obtain a true reading when using a refractometer on a fermented beverage because the presence of alcohol changes the instrument's calibration.

sack mead – The highest strength meads, typically with an original gravity of 1.120–1.170 and 14–18% ABV.

sanitize – To *reduce* the number of organisms (bacteria, yeast, etc.). Contrast to *sterilize*.

sparkling – Describes a carbonated mead. Sparkling mead should not gush from the bottle, but the carbonation can range from that like a typical beer to that of champagne.

specific gravity (SG) – A measurement that expresses the density of a liquid. Values less than 1.000 mean the liquid is less dense than pure water while values over 1.000 mean the liquid is denser than pure water. The specific gravity of an unfermented mead must expresses how much sugar is in the solution. For example, 1 gallon of a solution made from water and dissolved sugar that has a specific gravity of 1.046 has 1 pound of sugar in the gallon of solution.

staggered nutrient additions (SNA) – The periodic addition of essential nutrients during the initial portion of the fermentation.

standard mead – Meads of average strength, typically with an original gravity of 1.080–1.120 and 7.5–14% ABV.

starter – See *yeast starter*.

sterilize – To *remove* all organisms (bacteria, yeast, etc.). Sterilizing objects for mead-making is difficult and rarely done. Contrast to *sanitize*.

still – Describes a mead that is extremely low in carbonation. A still mead is not necessarily totally flat; it might have a few bubbles.

stuck fermentation – A situation in which a mead's final gravity is higher than anticipated.

structure – Usually refers to the combination of acidity and tannins in a mead.

tannins – In mead, bitter-tasting, organically occurring chemical compounds that have an astringent mouthfeel and can even become mouth-puckering at sufficient levels.

yeast – A single-cell organism that is responsible for fermentation. Most yeast strains used by mead-makers are members of the *Saccharomyces* genus and are either *S. cervesiae* or *S. bayanus*. Yeast is generally packaged as either a "dry" substance that needs to be rehydrated before use or as a liquid culture that may need to be used in a yeast starter to produce more cells.

yeast starter – The process of growing additional yeast in a controlled environment. See Chapter 7.

SAMPLE LOG PAGE

Batch Name: Cherry Pomegranate			
Mead Type: Melomel			
Description:			
Date: 9/8/13	Target Batch Size: 6 gallons	Target OG: 1.130	Target FG: 1.015 - 1.020
Water source and treatment: Filtered Eagan tap water			

INGREDIENTS

Amount	Ingredient	When Added
128 oz.	Old Orchard Pomegranate Juice (OG 1.074)	Initially
64 oz.	Langers Pomegranate (OG 1.074)	Initially
138 oz.	Indian Summer Montmorency Cherry Juice (OG 1.062)	Initially
	Clover honey to hit OG	Initially

Actual SG: 1.130	Actual Volume: 7.25

NUTRIENT MIXTURE

Total Amount	Nutrient Name
4 grams	Fermaid K
8 grams	Diammonium phosphate

STAGGERED NUTRIENT ADDITIONS

Amount	When Added	Other Notes	
¾ tsp	9/8/13	Initially	
¾ tsp	9/10/13 @ 16:00		
¾ tsp	9/12/13 @ 13:20		
¾ tsp	9/14/13 @ 17:15		

YEAST

Rehydration		
Yeast Strain: 71B-1122		Yeast Amount Used: 1 packet
Rehydration Nutrient: GoFerm		Rehydration Nutrient Amount: 5 grams
Rehydration Water Source: warm tap		Rehydration Water Amount: ~12 oz.
Rehydration Temperature:		104 F
Rehydration Start Time:		Rehydration End Time: 15 minutes

Yeast Starter							
Starter Size:				Starter Source:			

COMBINING YEAST WITH MUST

Yeast Temperature: 98F	Must Temperature: 72F
Temperature Difference: 26F	Atempering Steps:
Atemper Step Number:	When:
Atemper Step Number:	When:
Atemper Step Number:	When:

MEASUREMENTS

When	SG	Temperature	Other Notes
9/9/2013	1.138	68F	
9/10 @ 16:00	1.13	68F	Foamed
9/11/13 @ 11:00	1.096	68F	Little foam, effervescent
9/12/13 @ 13:00	1.072	71F	Still very active
9/13/13 @ 18:20	1.058	69F	
9/14/13 @ 17:15	1.038	69F	
9/15/13 @ 11:30	1.028	68F	
9/16/13 @ 11:00	1.02	67F	Still foam
9/17/13 @ 10:10	1.014	67F	
9/18/2013	1.012	67F	Rack to glass
11/7/2013	1.007		Rack to keg

ADJUSTMENTS

When	Amount	What Used	Other Comments	
9/9/2013	~1 gallon	filtered tap water	To hit OG of 1.130	

SOURCES

Brownwood Acres Foods (a source of fruit juice concentrate): www.brownwoodacres.com

Bulk quantities of Nekutli agave nectar: www.agavenectar.com

Fermentis yeast descriptions: www.fermentis.com/winemaking/product-range/activedry-wine-yeast/

Honey Locator (the National Honey Board's tool to locate suppliers of honey either by state or floral source): www.honey.com/honey-locator/

Honey Varietal Guides (by the National Honey Board): www.bjcp.org/mead/varietalguide pdf and www.honey.com/honey-at-home/learn-about-honey/honey-varietals
Lallemand/Lalvin yeast descriptions: www.lallemandwine.us/products/yeast_chart.php

Penzeys Spices (a good source for most spices): www.penzeys.com

PickYourOwn.org (find a pick-your-own farm near you): www.pickyourown.org/

Trader Joe's (a good source for mesquite honey): www.traderjoes.com

USDA Cooperative Extension System Offices (extension systems can help you find local growers of fruit and vegetables): www.csrees.usda.gov/Extension/

Vinter's Harvest yeast descriptions: vintnersharvest.com/collections/wine-yeasts

White Labs yeast descriptions: www.whitelabs.com/wine/home/listings

Wyeast Laboratories yeast descriptions: www.wyeastlab.com/he_m_yeaststrain.cfm and www.wyeastlab.com/hw_yeaststrain.cfm

PHOTO CREDITS

INDEX

Items in bold indicate a recipe. Page numbers in italics indicate an item that appears in a photograph or caption.

ABOUT THE AUTHOR

Steve Piatz is a retired electrical engineer who spent most of his career working as a software engineer. He is an award-winning mead- and beermaker and was the AHA Mead Maker of the Year in 2008. He is a member of both the Minnesota Homebrewers Association and the Saint Paul Homebrewers Club, a Grand Master V BJCP (Beer Judge Certification Program) judge, and an exam director for the BJCP. He resides in Eagan, Minnesota.

MORE GREAT BOOKS FROM VOYAGEUR PRESS

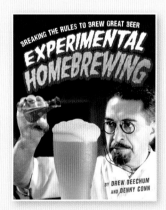

Experimental Homebrewing
(ISBN 978-0-7603-4538-2)

The Homebrew Journal
(ISBN 978-0-7603-4589-4)

*Craft Beer for
the Homebrewer*
(ISBN 978-0-7603-4474-3)